God, Let Me Out of This Marriage

God, Let Me Out of This Marriage

Denice Vickers
with Cliff Dudley

P.O. BOX 1045, HARRISON, ARK. 72601

first printing, July, 1981

© 1981 by New Leaf Press. All rights reserved. Printed in the United States of America. No part of this book may be used or reproduced in any manner whatsoever without written permission of the publisher except in the case of brief quotations in articles and reviews. For information write: New Leaf Press, Inc., P.O. Box 1045, Harrison, AR 72601.

Library of Congress Catalog Card Number: 80-83459
International Standard Book Number: 0-89221-080-x

Dedication

I dedicate this book to all those who are searching for an answer for their life—to the hurting and the tormented—and pray that in these pages you will see God is the Answer.

To my husband (Steve) whom I love and in whom I believe. I am awed by his walk with God and under God; Steve is my breath.

To mother who allowed me to open the pages of her life and whose cry for God became deep rooted in my own life.

Contents

	Dedication	v
1.	The Early Mold	9
2.	Increased Turmoil	16
3.	Changing Daddies	26
4.	Dating Young	35
5.	Getting Serious	44
6.	Stumbling into Marriage	56
7.	Suspicions	64
8.	Moving and Searching	77
9.	The Comforter	94
10.	Steve's Answer	102
11.	God, Let Me Out . . .	110
12.	Life and Death	117

1.
The Early Mold

"Come here, Lucky," I called. And my little white dog came running up to me. I would always know if he was happy or sad by looking at his tail. If it curled, I knew he was happy, but if it hung straight, I would go up to him and say, "Oh, Lucky, poor Lucky. You are so sad. Just like me."

During my happy times I acted like a little tomboy and would run outside without even a shirt on. When I started maturing, my older sister started complaining to mother how I was embarrassing her. I finally had to wear shirts.

During my sad times I would get alone with Lucky and tell him all about our problems. Every time mother and dad fussed, Lucky and I would have a little talk together.

I had no way of knowing then that these sad times in my life were going to mold my concept of God and men and marriage in such a way that I would live on the brink of disaster later on.

One day Lucky disappeared. I looked all over the neighborhood and thought I would cry my eyes out. I went to daddy because I thought he had gotten rid of Lucky, but daddy never did say. Until this day I don't know. But I remember feeling bitter because Lucky was my best friend.

When mom had married dad, mom thought he was the most wonderful thing in the world, that he could do no wrong. He would bring her a box of candy every payday. Mom had come from a home of truth and trust, and she thought life was just going to be perfect.

But mom started catching daddy in lies. One of the first lies concerned her engagement ring. Dad had told her that he paid three hundred dollars for it at the most expensive jewelry store in Birmingham, Alabama. After they were married, the diamond fell out, and mom took it back to the jewelry store to be put back in.

The man said, "Ma'am, your husband didn't get this here. All this is is a piece of glass."

One day when I was about three years old, mom's sister came to her and said, "Nellie, there are rumors out that Charles is having an affair."

Mom said, "I don't believe it. Not Charles." It wasn't long, however, until she began to notice that something was going on. This is when the torment began for her, the feeling that something was going on but that she could not prove it.

Dad also began saying cruel things to mom. Mom would be tormented and convinced that dad was right and that she had just been imagining evil thoughts about him. For a long time mother held her feelings inside, until finally she took a bus and went to a psychiatrist for help. He told her that she was on the verge of a nervous breakdown.

Mom had been a good Christian before she married daddy, but daddy did not want her to go to church or read her Bible. He put her down about it, so she made the mistake many women do and sent us kids to church while she stayed home with dad. She had developed a growing fear that if she went to church with us kids, daddy might go off with another woman while she was at church. She was secure as long as she was at home with him.

The only time I remember daddy ever going to church with us was the Sunday I had on a little red dotted swiss dress with a white collar. I was so happy to be between mother and daddy in church and to lay my head in mother's lap. I would throw my collar over my face so I could suck my thumb without anybody seeing me.

Daddy was a real country-type man and didn't have much education. He had quit school when he was in the elementary grades. However, he was a hard worker and the type of man who was going to be successful in anything he did. That was his personality.

In church that morning, I was sucking my thumb with the collar pulled up over my face thinking that nobody would see me. The congregation was singing, "Bringing in the Sheaves." But daddy, instead of singing the right words and going through the trouble of reading the songbook, sang, "Bringing in the cheese, bringing in the cheese; Here Columbus, Georgia, bringing in the cheese."

I remember sitting there thinking, *I wonder why daddy won't sing the right words.* But that was just daddy.

Mother and daddy were both real hard workers. Because mother worked, we had maids. Back then a maid did not cost much money. We were not rich, but it was not hard to afford to have someone clean the house.

One day I walked into the den and saw daddy on the sofa with a woman who lived two doors down from us. She had on white short shorts and a blue cotton shirt. I was standing at the door, and they didn't know I was there. She was taking a throw pillow and teasing him with it, and I saw them laughing and hugging. I didn't understand why.

I went into the kitchen and asked our maid, "Why is my daddy hugging on that woman?"

Her answer was, "Denice, go outside and play and don't ask any questions."

Later the maid told the neighbor, and that neighbor came and told my mother. Mother and the neighbor got me aside and questioned me as to what I saw. So I told them.

Daddy, of course, gave mother a good excuse. He would

always tell mother, "Nellie, you're crazy. You're just imagining all this."

Mother was having such horrible nerve trouble from all the torment that she would convince herself, "Yeah, I'm just imagining it." Mother could not leave daddy.

Daddy was off and away from home because of his job. I remember nights when mom would be in her bed crying and saying, "God, help me. Lord, please help me." I always wondered why God wouldn't help her. I realize now that she didn't know how to let God help her.

As a child, I also had a hunger for God. I thought about God so much that in my childish eyes I thought, *Oh, maybe I'm going to be another Jesus or one of God's special people.*

Mom tried to raise us with strict morals. She taught us how important it was that we keep ourselves clean. If we ever said the word "shoot," we would get a spanking for cussing. We would say, "Mom, that's not cussing."

She would retort, "It's a slang word."

Mother always demanded that we respect daddy, and she always praised him to us. She told us how he was a good worker and a good provider. But we kids knew that daddy was running around, and we saw how mother was hurting. And in our minds we didn't like daddy because we couldn't trust him. We started seeing mother as good and dad, bad.

He was on a constant search for something that was lacking in his life. He tried to find it in women and in money. I don't believe it was that he didn't love mother and us kids, but rather that Jesus was missing from his life.

During our good times together, mother would come home from work and cook supper. She would sing and laugh while she cooked. We would all stand around in the kitchen and tell her about the events of the day. Mom would always act like everything we had to say was so important. We would discuss our friends' problems with her, and she would give us advice for them. To me, mom seemed so wise. She would always tell us how beautiful we were and how proud she was of us.

Every time we were around her, she would try to put in our minds something about the Lord. She kept repeating over and over, "Denice, God is the answer. God is the answer." That thought stayed with me even through the crises later on in my life. She knew God was the answer all right, but she did not know *how* He could be the answer.

She didn't know *how* He could be her psychiatrist. She didn't know that the Bible said not to seek ungodly counsel. Her psychiatrist had told her, "Nellie, you take life too seriously. You need to have more fun. You need to have an affair with a man. You shouldn't think of God so much."

In the middle of all the torment mother was going through with daddy and the psychiatrist, she still tried to make life happy for us kids. When I was a child, it seemed that I was talking all the time. I laughed very much and acted rather silly. Mom said that every morning when I was a child, I woke up laughing.

By the time I was in third grade, my talking and laughing were getting me in trouble in school. The teacher would spank me in class and one time threatened, "Denice, if you don't stop that laughing, I cannot teach you." So she brought me up in front of the class and turned me over in her lap and spanked me.

Oh, my boyfriend is watching me get a spanking, I thought.

Then the teacher said, "You have so many petticoats on, I'll bet you didn't even feel this."

I sat down embarrassed and with hurt feelings because I felt the teacher was making fun of my petticoats that were so important to me.

Sometimes the teacher would even draw a circle on the blackboard and get me to stick my nose in it to try to make me stop laughing. I suppose deep down the reason I laughed so much was to keep from crying. I think that's why Denice was so silly. Yet even today I enjoy a good laugh or silly thought.

The teacher tried everything to calm me down. She even made me sit out in the hallway on a stool with a sign that said, "Baby," and a little hat on my head.

But as it turned out, I ended up her favorite student. I didn't realize that until Halloween day, when we were going to get out of school early so we could have a carnival. I made up my mind that morning, *I'm not going to laugh. I'm going to be real quiet so that she won't make me stay after school.* All day I sat real quiet in school.

When the bell rang, the teacher said, "Everybody can leave but Denice."

I thought to myself, *Oh, I was so good today.* I wanted to leave too and make my costume.

I felt hurt and couldn't understand why I was being punished; I had been so good that day. The teacher went out of the room, and I sat by myself.

Soon she came back with two cokes in her hand—one for her and one for me. She handed me my coke and said, "Now, you're going to help me decorate today." That's when I realized that she enjoyed my company, and one of the reasons I was staying after school so much was that she enjoyed my talking with her while she was grading papers. I wouldn't shout. I would just sit and rattle on.

I thought she was an old maid, yet now that I look back, I realize she wasn't that old but was beautiful and was just waiting to marry—which she later did. The teacher once told my mother, "Of all my students, I can tell that Denice is going to marry early." I guess she could see that I was boy crazy.

Yes, I was happy and silly and boy crazy, but that could not cover the turmoil that I saw in our house. Mother and daddy fought more and more often at home.

One night daddy had mother on the floor and was hitting her in the face. The fight had started with her accusing him of having an affair with another woman. "You know you are; why don't you admit it?" she yelled at him as they wrestled.

The fights at home were often sparked by daddy's antics outside the home. Daddy was a salesman and seemed to always have to be noticed. Once at a company picnic daddy got a hula skirt and a top and put them on. While the jukebox played, he did the hula. I was proud because everyone was looking at my daddy. I thought, *Everybody is laughing. My daddy is making people laugh.* Yet, I also felt sick to my stomach because I felt that he was trying to get the women to look at him. Mother would sit there and be a good wife and laugh with everyone else.

Things got worse. One day mother took thirty sleeping pills in an attempt to commit suicide. She didn't really want to die. She told daddy what she had done and tried to get him to call an ambulance, but he wouldn't do it. So my oldest sister Janice ran across the street and got a neighbor to call the ambulance.

When the ambulance people were putting mother into the ambulance, daddy looked at her coldly and said, "I hope you die."

Mother became more and more suspicious of daddy's actions. She would look at and smell daddy's clothes, hoping to find some evidence to support her suspicions. She looked for makeup on his collar, the smell of perfume on his clothes, anything to prove that he was not faithful to her. By the time he would come home, she had worked herself into a state of torment and was ready to start arguing with him. They would fuss and scream, and then daddy would get mad and start throwing her around the room. When we saw this, we would start crying. Janice, Pam, and I would beg, "Daddy, please quit, quit!"

Mother would scream, "Go get help! Call the police!"

One of those times, Janice and I ran across the back yard to the neighbors' house. We knocked on the door. My heart was beating wildly, and I yelled, "Daddy's killing mama."

The neighbors called the police, but by the time they got there, the fight was over. The police talked to daddy and mother. They then asked mama, "Well, do you want to file something against him?"

Her answer was, "No, not this time."

Mother would often have a black eye and go to work and fake walking into a door or something. However, most people by this time were not asking questions—they knew.

Mother would often sing songs about God while working or resting. That was her way to try to find peace. But peace was not to come that easily into our household.

2.
Increased Turmoil

Despite all the anguish and quarreling and dissension that my parents had, we children still had a fun-filled childhood. We had happiness but little joy.

On Friday nights we would have our girlfriends over to spend the night. We would go roller-skating and then come back and watch "Shock Theater" on TV. Pam, my other older sister, would always hide under the covers and say, "Tell me when the scary part is over." Mom would make fudge for us to eat while we watched the program.

During the summer we were permitted to join the swimming club. It cost around thirty-five dollars, which in those days was a lot of money. But mom would call every year and talk with the manager and say, "Could we join and then I'll pay it out a couple of dollars a week until the bill is paid?" The manager always said yes. I felt a little ashamed that we just didn't have the money to pay. But that feeling would end as soon as I took my first dive into the pool.

Being a giggler was not always good when I went swimming. Many times when I would get into the deep part of the pool and get tickled, I would laugh so hard that I would start drowning and the lifeguard would have to come and drag me back to the lifeguard station. They even threatened that if I didn't stop laughing in the pool, they were going to forbid me to go into the deep end anymore.

Our house was on a hill, and that made roller-skating very easy, except that I didn't know how to stop once I got going down the hill. Instead of stopping with my feet, I would simply sit down. So almost every night my mother would have to pull my pants down and doctor my "hiney" which was inflamed and bleeding. Mother would say, "Denice, why in the world are you tearing your rear end up? Why don't you learn how to stop some other way?"

"Don't worry, mom; it's all right. It doesn't hurt that much," I would say.

One day I decided to get a pillow and fasten it to the back of my seat with one of daddy's belts to hold it on. One of the neighbors called my mother and was laughing uncontrollably. In between chuckles she said, "I've got to tell you what your daughter is doing. She's outside with a pillow tacked to her rear end, and when she's at top speed she sits down on the pillow."

Several years went by, and we moved to a larger house off of the hill. It was large enough that we could have parties. Pam and Janice, my older sisters, would plan various parties— a Hawaiian party, a hillbilly party, or something of that sort. We would dress up in different costumes, invite all the kids that we knew, have a record player, and have a lot of fun.

One time when I was in the fifth grade and Pam was in the sixth grade, a boy named Tommy Vickers came to the party. He was also in the sixth grade and had a crush on Pam. It seemed that all the boys had a crush on her. She seemed to have so much confidence in herself, and the boys really liked that. I had a super crush on Tommy. I thought he was so cute, and when I heard that he was coming to one of our parties, I was really excited. That night at the party we decided to play spin the bottle. Whoever the bottle pointed to got a kiss from the person spinning the bottle. I had never kissed a boy in my life.

It was time for Tommy Vickers to spin the bottle. I was standing there with my heart pounding and was hoping, *Oh, I just hope it lands on me.* He gave the bottle a good spin. I'm sure he was hoping that it would land on Pam, just as all the other boys hoped when they spun the bottle. But, believe it or not, the bottle pointed to me.

We had fixed it up so that if the bottle pointed to you, you had to go into Janice's bedroom and kiss in the bedroom so that no one would see you kiss. I immediately saw the disappointment on Tommy's face when the bottle pointed to me. But I didn't care.

We went back to Janice's bedroom where it was rather dark, except for the street light shining through the window. He just could not bring himself to kiss me. He stood there and looked out the window, dreading the next move. So I stood there looking out the window with him. He started acting like he was going to walk out the door. I wasn't going to let him get away with that, so I said, "Well, Tommy, aren't you going to kiss me?"

He turned to me shyly and said, "Yeah."

When he kissed me, I thought I went straight to Heaven. I was walking on the clouds.

That night after the party was over, I was lying on the bed listening to Pam and Janice and our girlfriends talking about all the boys who were at the party. Janice turned to me and said, "Well, if you think Tommy's cute, you should see his older brother Steve."

I said, *"No way! Nobody is as cute as Tommy Vickers."*

Steve was very popular at school, but my mind was on Tommy. However, soon Tommy went on to junior high and I forgot about him.

While we still lived in this larger house, we had one fabulous Christmas. Daddy seemed to turn into a little boy at Christmas, and he made Christmas so much fun. He made reindeer and Santa Clauses and put Christmas trees in the living room and bedroom. He bought mother clothes, three pairs of shoes, and handbags to match. This was more than he had ever done before.

I thought, "I wonder why daddy is doing this? Is this going to be our last Christmas with him, or is he doing this because of his guilt?"

I was the baby of the family for nine years and enjoyed every minute of the attention as baby. One day mother came home from the doctor and an afternoon of shopping and held up a maternity dress. She made the announcement that she was expecting. It wasn't long until I had a baby sister, Lee Ann. And a year and a half later I had a baby brother, Charles.

All during this time, we believed daddy was still having an affair. The fighting was getting worse and worse. Mother was throwing things at him. I remember the night she threw the iron, and it hit a lamp and broke it.

The doctor that mother was seeing had her on nerve pills, but nothing seemed to help.

The worst quarreling happened on the weekends, and we began dreading the thought of another weekend coming. We knew that a quarrel was going to happen. We older girls got into the habit of going roller-skating because we knew that we had to get out of the house. Yet the whole time we were skating, we wondered if we were going to come home and find someone dead. We knew that mom and dad would never have killed each other on purpose, as they weren't like that. But we were afraid that in their fussing and fighting there might be an accident.

At school I occupied myself with being a cheerleader. My sister Janice was a cheerleading teacher and chose the cheerleaders. Although I was not very coordinated, and perhaps should not have been a cheerleader, I was chosen.

In spite of our school activities, we always had the fear that one day mother would be successful at suicide or get hurt seriously when they were fighting.

One night Pam, Janice, and I were standing out on our driveway talking. A neighbor had invited Janice to come spend the night. However, Janice had always been the one who helped break up the fights between mother and dad.

I was the type of child who wouldn't show what was bothering me. I would feel more inside than I was expressing. I felt fear in the pit of my stomach. Yet I would act as though it didn't bother me. Pam often cried and would get very emotional about the fights. But Janice would get in there and try to break up the fights.

As we were standing in the driveway, mother and dad began fighting again. It was a weekend, and we knew that all "hell was going to break loose." Pam and I started begging Janice, "Please don't spend the night at the neighbors. Who's going to stop them from killing each other?" So Janice told the neighbor that she couldn't come.

Although Pam was only a child, she stood there staring straight ahead and said, "I hope they kill each other. I hope this time that they'll kill each other and it will all be over." We were frightened and getting sick and tired of the situation.

To make matters worse, the psychiatrist had told mother that in her state of mind, if she were to kill her husband, no court would ever convict her. Every so often mother would go to the hospital for shock treatments to help her "cope" with her situation.

For awhile after the shock treatments, things would not bother her as much. I would think, *Oh, boy, mother's going to come home and not be bothered.*

The effect of the shock treatment seemed to wear off quickly. Things began bothering her again. During all of this daddy would look at her and laugh. He'd say, "You're going crazy. It's all in your mind. It's all in your mind."

Then mama would think, "I'm just imagining this. It is all in my mind." Daddy convinced her because he was a good liar—really good.

Mother always looked at us kids with much love. I could see the love in her and how she was hating what we were going through. Yet, she was so wrapped up in her nerve problems that she was kind of helpless.

As time went on, we rented out our big house and moved to a smaller home. It was a real cheap house. We went from a real nice home to a home worse than we'd ever been in before. I could tell that daddy was losing interest in what we lived in. It seemed to be the type of home where we would have a roof over our heads but little more. He was so wrapped up in his "love affair" that he didn't seem to care about us anymore.

As small as I was, I tried to take matters into my own hands. I would go over to the house of my girlfriend Melissa and call the lady with whom daddy was having an affair. When she would answer the phone, I would say, "You leave my daddy alone!"

She covered up the phone, but I could hear her say, "Charles, it's Denice."

Then she got back on the phone and talked real sweetly, "Honey, I'm not seeing your daddy. Your daddy's not here."

I said, "I just heard you talking to daddy. He's there. You leave him alone!" I'd cry and hang up.

I didn't tell mother about this because I knew that then she would know for a fact. Mother would call the lady's husband and say, "Your wife is having an affair with my husband."

The other man just thought mother was nuts and would say, "You're just thinking that. My wife is not being unfaithful to me."

But mother kept insisting, "I'm telling you, she's having an affair with my husband."

When mother became pregnant with my little brother Charlie, daddy said that he wanted her to have an abortion. This was during a time when abortions were almost unheard of. Mother told him that it was out of the question.

Mother was pregnant, and so was daddy's other lady friend. The day mother went into labor and went to the hospital, daddy was too busy to take her. So a neighbor took her. After mother gave birth to Charlie, they took her into a room and said, "Oh, there was a friend of yours here last week." They told mother who it was. "She had a little boy in this same room."

Mother started screaming, "I don't want to be in this room! Get me out of this room right now!" They had to take her to another room.

I remember thinking, "Is that other little boy that was

born also one of my brothers? Is that daddy's child?" Later I realized that he wasn't, because he looked just like his real dad and not like my father. But he could have been.

During this time Janice, Pam, and I were all boy crazy. Boys were always hanging out at the house. They were not allowed to come in the house unless mom was home, but we could stand out in the yard and talk with them. They all loved mom. For our age we had much freedom—probably more than we should have had. But mom always said that she didn't feel that she enjoyed her teens as much as she should have. So she gave us more freedom.

Mom trusted us so much that we never wanted to disappoint her.

It seemed that I was the first girl in every grade to try something new. I was the first girl to get my ears pierced and wear lipstick. I did things earlier than I should have, but it was because mother allowed us to have freedom. I think she was trying to make up to us because of what we were going through at home. We felt such love from mother; she was so good that all of us kids would not have lied to her or hurt her for anything in the world.

Because mother was so good and loyal to us, we knew that no matter what happened, we would never lose her and that she would never do us wrong.

One time the whole family took a trip with daddy. We stayed at a motel with a swimming pool. The second we stopped at the motel, all of us kids went swimming. We were staying in a housekeeping cottage and daddy would leave the motel to go to work.

Mother went into the bathroom and turned on the gas, waiting once again for death to come. She had even plugged up the cracks in the bathroom door with towels, trying to keep the gas in the bathroom. When daddy came back, he kicked the door in and saved her life. Later she had to go into the hospital because she had developed pneumonia.

The nurses asked her why she wanted to do something like that—didn't she love her children?

Mother started crying and looked up into their faces, saying over and over, "You just don't understand. You just don't understand."

We girls thought, *It's daddy. It's daddy.*

All of this made me think more and more that all men were bad. I remember looking at mother and seeing her face filled with fear and anger. I don't believe mom really wanted to kill herself. She just wanted to make dad wake up to what he was doing.

We finally moved out of the house we were renting and into another home. However, we were still renting out the real nice home that we used to live in.

The fights were going on all the time, mostly on weekends though because daddy did not work on Saturdays and Sundays. If there was not a physical fight, mom and dad would sling words back and forth at each other. We children would go into the bedroom, sit on the bed, and talk about our boyfriends. We would act as if nothing was going on. We would hear screaming, but we would sit and talk about our boyfriends or plan a party for the weekend. Mother would let us have girlfriends over to spend the night. They would hear the screaming going on in the other room and would say, "How do you stand this?"

We would laugh and say, "Oh, we're used to it." We would pass over it lightly, but inside we were dying.

While the fighting and screaming continued, we continued to plan parties. We would call Jane and get her to bring the potato chips. Johnny would bring the soft drinks. If we heard it getting real bad, with daddy beating mother or mother throwing things, we would know it was time to stop the party.

Fortunately for us children, daddy was not a drinker. I remember thinking, *At least he has high morals.* It seemed strange; here he was having an affair, and I was thinking he had high morals because he didn't drink. I realize now that the main reason he didn't drink was because he had bad ulcers. He often went to the kitchen cabinet, took out a box of baking soda, poured it into his hand, and licked the baking soda out of his hand. He said that it made his ulcers feel better.

Daddy was a natural cutup. He was fun to be around

when he was not fighting with mom. The best time for all of us would be when we would take a vacation to the beach. We children looked forward to going to the beach in the summer to play in the sand and be free. And even mommy and daddy did not fight as much when we were on vacation.

Yet, strange things continued to happen even on a trip. One summer at the beach daddy put on his shorts and walked around barechested and said to us kids, "Now on the beach don't you call me daddy. Just call me Uncle Charlie." He laughed, and mother said he was kidding. But deep within me I felt hurt that he wanted me to call him uncle instead of daddy.

He got out a can of blond hair spray, lightened his hair, and I guess thought he looked better on the beach walking around with blond hair rather than brown. I kept asking myself, *Why is he doing this? What is the reason for all of this?*

As a girl I was starved for my dad's love. He hardly ever touched me. Most of the time I didn't even think he even knew my name. By the time there were five of us kids, when he wanted something, he would call me Pam or Janice. He never seemed to get my name right. Yet, I knew he knew my name. He treated all of us kids that way. I would answer to any name that he called me.

Pam was the type of girl who would say, "Daddy, hug me, hold me." And then he would cuddle her, and she would cuddle up against him.

I'd think to myself, "Oh, I wish I could do like Pam and ask daddy to hug me." But I couldn't. Inside me I would be wanting to be brave enough to ask daddy, "Could I sit next to you?" But I would just act like it didn't matter.

I was the type of child who would act like it didn't really matter. Then I would laugh it off. But, again, within me I was dying. That carried into my adulthood so that later I couldn't express myself.

The only time I remember daddy ever really touching me was the night Pam, Janice, and I had gone to a baseball game. We had the coaches, who were only a little bit older than we were, drive us home. Mother and daddy had always told us never to get a ride with anybody, that they would come and get us. But this particular night we needed a ride home and asked the coaches to give us the ride, thinking that mother and daddy were not coming after us.

Mom and dad came to pick us up and found a deserted baseball field. They were told, "Your girls left with the coaches."

When mother heard "coaches," she thought they were grown men. By the time we walked in the door, they didn't give us a chance to explain who the boys were. They had worried about grown men hurting us.

Daddy lined all three of us up and made us bend over for a spanking. I saw his hand and his lifeline coming at me. When it hit, I thought, *Oh, that feels so good! He loves me! He's spanking me! He loves me! He cares whether or not I get hurt.* That was the first time I felt that daddy loved me. He touched me. He cared.

Mother continued to have nerve troubles, and when I went to her to be friendly or to get attention, I would pat her on the arm. She would say, "Oh, Denice, don't touch me. Don't touch me. If you only knew how much it hurts." Her nerves were so sensitive on her skin. As a consequence, I wasn't able to express my love to anyone through touching.

She would be so tired from working all day and cooking. She loved us and wanted love, but she just could not take it. I ended up feeling insecure and would go to my room and sometimes suck my thumb.

3.
Changing Daddies

All of a sudden I seemed to grow up. By the time I was thirteen and in the seventh grade, I was dating.

Day after day I would watch mother play detective when daddy wasn't around. She would examine his collars and search his clothes for evidence. She would smell them for perfume. She would go through his wallet. Her torment seemed like a living hell. No matter what the evidence, daddy would continue to say, "Oh, you're just imagining all this." This would only add to the torment.

One night she went outside and searched the car for evidence. She went through the car like a crazy person. Then she found it—a green thread. Yes, nothing but a green thread. To mother that was all the proof she needed, a green thread. She walked into the house and stared at it. (Somehow I knew then that green thread would change my life and return to haunt me.)

She went to daddy and screamed, "Look at this! Look at this green thread." Then she said, "This belongs to the other woman, doesn't it?"

The effects of this episode and of all the fighting went right to the pit of my stomach, and I'd get sick. I wouldn't express my feelings. I would not cry, scream, or say a word. Mother never knew that it was even bothering me. I'd go in my bedroom and lie on the bed, suck my thumb, and feel content. As long as I sucked my thumb, I didn't mind, and the hurt would go away. I sucked my thumb for a long time. That was my outlet—my thumb.

I couldn't express myself as well as Janice and Pam could. Mom and dad never knew. They thought that sweet little Denice who never caused trouble, who never asked for anything, who always took the hand-me-down clothes from the older sisters, who never required anything didn't even know what was going on. I never required anything but just to live and eat and have my thumb—don't take my thumb.

While we were living on Bradley Drive, Janice and Pam came to me and said, "We're tired of this. We're going to mother and ask her to divorce daddy. Are you with us? We're tired of their fighting every time we have company. One of these days they're going to kill themselves. We're tired of calling the police and seeing the blue lights turning in front of the house. We're embarrassed."

I simply agreed.

We went to mama and said, "Mama, we're tired of all this, and we want you to raise us. We don't want daddy to raise us. We're tired of him." (Mother had been married to daddy twenty years, and she really loved him.)

Janice continued, "Mother, Denice, Pam, and I have decided that we don't want daddy in the house anymore. We want just you. We're tired of daddy hurting you, and we want him to leave."

Then mother said, "Are you sure? Are you sure this is what you want?" She looked at all of us, waiting for our answer.

We all said, "Yes."

Then she went to daddy and told him to get some clothes and leave. That night while mama was at work, daddy got all his clothes and left. He moved into an apartment.

It wasn't long until his girlfriend's husband called mother and said that he was suspicious—after all these years of mother telling him, "Your wife is fooling around with my husband," and his reply always being, "You're nuts. You're just imagining it."

Shortly after that mother and the other woman's husband caught daddy and his girlfriend. Divorces quickly followed, and daddy married the other woman. She gave up her two children for daddy; however, their marriage did not last very long and ended in another divorce.

Mother had lived a life of torment in her mind and hadn't realized how Satan was trying to destroy her life. Now she had to readjust to a new way of living.

We lived in a little two bedroom home on Bradley Drive and converted the living room into a third bedroom. Here we were—a mother with five children. Charlie was only two years old; Lee Ann was only four. I was in the seventh grade; Pam, in the eighth; and Janice, in the tenth.

Soon the bill collectors started calling and threatening. Our lights were turned off, and the phone was disconnected several times. We would come home and discover that we had no water because mother had no money to pay the bill.

In the meantime daddy had bought a nice home and had furnished it elegantly. I went there one time while he was married to the other woman. He had beautiful new furniture, and he and his new wife were acting so happy. They didn't seem to have any financial problems, but *we* were having it rough!

But never once did daddy's new home look good enough for me to want to go and live with him. Being with mother was home.

All of this turmoil really took its toll on my life. I began to think that all men, especially fathers, ran around with other women. Most of my girlfriends' parents were divorced or one or both parents were having affairs. I didn't have any friends who had good homes.

Things became increasingly desperate around home. It seemed that as soon as mom got the divorce, everything in the house started falling apart. The sink got a hole in it. The TV knobs fell off, and the only way we could change channels was to use the prongs of a fork.

One day I tried to surprise mother by waxing the kitchen floor. I started moving the china cabinet, and when I did, all the china fell out and broke. I called mama at work and said, "Mama, I busted your china."

"How many pieces?" she asked.

"All of them!" I cried.

She began weeping and said, "Can't I have anything? Can't I have anything?"

I hung up the phone and lay across the bed and cried and cried and cried. The china was just about all mother had left because everything else in her life was falling apart.

With dad no longer around, mother started reading the Bible to us every morning at the breakfast table. We often laughed because it always seemed to open to the passage that said, "Children, obey your parents."

Mom would laugh and say, "That's right."

One day Janice came to mom and said, "Mom, Micky and I are going to get married. We are going to Georgia because Micky's mom won't sign for him. I want you to go with us."

Mom screamed out, "No, Janice, you're too young!"

I ran to the kitchen to see what was wrong and saw mom staring at two determined sixteen-year-old kids. She realized that they were going to get married with or without her consent, and she finally said, "I'll go with you."

Micky said, "My father lives in Florida, and he will sign for us since my mother won't."

"Well, get your daddy to come and sign," mother replied.

Bill, Micky's dad, came right away, and he and mother took the children to Georgia to be married. Bill was a well built and very handsome man. On the journey to Georgia he and mother talked about how they could help the newlyweds get established. By the time they returned from the wedding in Georgia, Bill had decided to move to Montgomery.

He started courting mother immediately, and we kids were excited. We watched mother and could tell she felt so pretty—a man was looking at her. We could all tell the difference in her. She would sing and laugh around the house, and it was wonderful seeing her like this. Mom was a beautiful woman; now she was going to have someone who would appreciate her.

Bill and mother had a short courtship and were soon married. Mother knew that Bill had been an alcoholic at one time, but not knowing anything about alcoholics, she assumed he would never be one again.

Almost as soon as the honeymoon was over, everything again started going downhill because Bill started drinking again. He didn't want mother to see him when he was drinking, so he would go to a boarding house. He would come back every other day or sometimes stay longer. He was still kind and sweet. I'd talk to him about God and say that God could help him stop drinking, but I really didn't know if or how God would.

I would sit on the arm of the chair and touch his ear, trying to tell him that I appreciated him and loved him. He liked us and would chase us kids around the house with a coat hanger on his head, pretending to be a monster. We'd scream and laugh.

He'd go up to my little brother and say, "Your name is Sally."

He'd cry and say, "No, I'm named Charlie."

During this period mother's daddy died and left her a couple thousand dollars. She was a bookkeeper, and Bill was an accountant. So she thought that if she could get him into a business, it would help him stop drinking, especially if he had a goal in life. Mother rented a little office building and took the money and started a business. But Bill never showed up at work.

Mother had quit her job, and they both were going to do bookkeeping. But the job folded, and she lost all the money that she'd inherited. She cried many nights and prayed to God for help.

Mother became increasingly despondent and seemed to let us kids do things without her thinking. I was hardly fifteen and didn't have a driver's license, and yet she'd let me drive the car. One such time I took my little sister and brother to the "Y" to watch a football game. And coming back, I had an accident.

My brother wasn't hurt, but my little sister was really banged up and cut her nose on the dashboard. My real father happened to be right behind us and was the first one to arrive at the car. He took us home and fussed over us, and in the midst of all of this confusion, I couldn't help thinking how wonderful it was that my father had paid attention to us.

After the divorce, we hardly ever saw him. He was always saying that he had tried to see us or that he had tried to bring us ice cream or that he had tried to do this or that; yet we knew he wasn't really telling the truth, because we were always home. How I longed for daddy to come home and pay a little attention to us.

While we were in school, Pam and I became quite popular. We were elected by the school board to be the "Miss Charming" at the Valentine dance—Pam for the ninth grade and I for the eighth grade. When the voting was finished, we were immediately called into the gym and told that we could not accept the awards because our grades were too bad. We did not have the required B average. I just sat there stunned. It seemed as though we simply could not win anything. Everything was against us.

Of course, when I look back now, I know I wasn't a good student. I never really learned how to study. All I cared about were the boys. I was totally boy crazy. I spent all my time at school, planning what I would do on the weekends.

Janice had left home and married at sixteen. And one day shortly after that Pam walked into the house and said, "I'm quitting school—I'm going to get married."

When I went to school the next day, all the cliques were buzzing. And I knew what they were thinking; they all thought that both of my sisters *had* to get married.

An avalanche seemed to be falling on my mother. First the divorce. Then my one sister getting married. Now my other.

And I went to Pam and said, "Please, don't get married."

She looked at me and said, "Denice, I am going to get married. I've just had it."

I looked at her very soberly and replied, "Well, Janice might have gotten married, and now you; but I'm telling you one thing—I'm not going to. Not me. Not until I'm at least twenty-one."

Pam looked at me and said, "Denice, you're going to eat those words. You're going to fall in love, and you'll want to get married too."

"Not me; I'm not falling in love." And yet here I was, probably one of the most boy crazy teenagers around.

Our house was always full of teenagers. Mom would invite them in and make them feel at home. We'd sit around the table and talk. And I was so proud when the kids would say, "You're so lucky to have a mother like that." And I really knew that I was lucky, because mother had such compassion and so much love to give. And our boyfriends would all come to mother for counselling. But they never saw the other side: the torment, the anguish, the pain that she seemingly suffered twenty-four hours a day. No one could see the torment because mom kept it inside and worked hard at being happy on the outside.

Now I was the oldest girl at home. With Pam and Janice married, it was my job to keep the lawn cut and fix anything that needed fixing. I tried to be the "man" around the house, keeping things in order.

One day one of the girls who was walking by the house saw me mowing the lawn and said, "I can't believe this—that cute little Denice Perkins would be cutting the grass."

I said, "Aw, think nothing of it; I've done this all of my life."

The other girl had always lived in an apartment, and she asked me, "Denice, could I cut the grass?"

I thought to myself, *This is fantastic! This kid wants to cut the grass!* So I let her cut the whole yard while I drank tea and watched her.

Her name was Robin. From that day on we became very good friends, along with another girlfriend of hers called C.Y. We did crazy things together and shared wonderful times.

Once Robin confessed to me that she had never kissed a boy, and I then proceeded to tell her just exactly how to do it. We all had fun talking "girl talk," and I just absolutely knew she needed to get over the fear of kissing.

We were planning to go to a dance and knew a certain boy was going to give us a ride home. I said, "Now when he starts to kiss you, don't panic." And I explained to her just what to do. It was so much fun as she stood at the door with the boy and I peeked out the window and watched. When I finally saw them kiss, I was almost as excited as Robin who came screaming in the door, "I did it! I did it!"

From that time on she was either spending the night at my house, or I was over at her house. My mother became like a mother to Robin.

Even though my stepfather, Bill, did not live at the house, he did manage to come by for breakfasts. One morning Bill didn't show up. We were somewhat worried, especially mother, but she had to go on to work, and I went to school.

Robin and I happened to be at the principal's office when the phone rang, and they wanted to speak to Denice Perkins. The girl called my name out over the loudspeaker. I said, "I'm right here."

She turned to me and said, "Denice, this phone call's for you."

I went around the desk and picked up the phone. It was my mother, and she said, "Your daddy's dead . . . and I'll be by to pick you up in a minute." I could tell she was really upset.

I screamed, "Mother, which daddy? Who's dead—daddy or Bill?" But she had already hung up before I knew.

I sat there trying to decide who I wanted to be dead. Did I want it to be my real father, or did I want it to be Bill? Both of them had been such a burden to my life. Yet deep down I knew I loved my daddy the most.

When I got into the car, I asked, "Mama, mama,

who's dead?"

She said, "Denice, it's Bill." She had gone to the boarding house and couldn't get him to respond. She found him lying in the bed. He had hemorrhaged to death in his sleep.

Mom always kicked her leg up and sang. That was mom.

4.
Dating Young

As time passed, it seemed that my life revolved more and more around boys. I really thought my love life was looking up when a boy from Lanier High School (where the upper class kids went) asked me to go out on a double date.

Shortly after he picked me up, it became obvious that the couple in the back seat was only interested in petting and necking heavily. I was burned up. Even though I dated young, I had always maintained high moral standards. And the more they petted, the angrier I got.

We went to a drive-in, and I was determined to watch the movie. My date kept staring at me and wanting to "make out." I could see him out of the corner of my eye while I watched the movie. He was just making me "sick at my stomach," thinking he could start slobbering all over me. Then I realized that the only reason he had asked me out was so that he could "make out."

I finally turned to him and said, "Do you have a problem?"

And he said, "Are you going to watch this movie?"

I answered with a question. "Donny, when you called me tonight, what did you say when you got me on the phone?"

He said, "I called you and said, 'Denice, do you want to go out tonight?'"

I then asked, "Where did you tell me you'd take me?"

"I told you I'd take you to the movie," he replied.

I said, "If you wanted to take me out and make out, why didn't you call me and say, 'Do you want to go and make out?'"

And he said, "Because you wouldn't have gone."

I said, "You're exactly right!"

Then he said, "Well, I'm taking you home!" He cranked up the car, and the couple in the back seat never knew that we had left the drive-in.

My mother always had a rule that when I dated a boy, he had to walk me to the door. Well, mother heard the car drive up. She was looking out the window and saw that he was not walking me to the door. So she headed out to bawl him out. I knew why she was coming.

I opened the car door, turned around, and said, "Don't bother walking me to the door." *Why should he start being a gentleman now,* I thought.

Mama came to me and said, "Now wait a minute, Denice!" She was going to talk to my date for not walking me to the door.

I said, "Mama, just wait; don't say anything. Let's go in the house. I want to talk to you."

Just then Donny screeched off with his car. I got a chance to tell her why he brought me home. She was really proud of me and glad that I did what I did.

At the time, I was also dating a boy who was much older than I was. I was fourteen and Denny was about eighteen. He was a very good boy, and he respected me. That's why I enjoyed dating him. He liked me just the way I was, and he was a gentleman. I also liked dating him because he had a car, and it was a way to get back and forth to the skating rink. Many times Denny would put his arm around me and try to squeeze me. He'd say, "Why won't you ever kiss me?"

And I'd say, "I just don't want to. I don't want to kiss you." We were even going steady, but I didn't want to kiss just to be kissing. I wanted it to mean something when I kissed a boy.

One day I decided to break up with him. After we broke up, I started going to the "Y" dances with Robin and C.Y.

As I was younger, I had often heard Janice and Pam talking with their girlfriends in the bedroom. Janice was always the one giving advice. She was the "Dear Abby" and "Ann Landers" to all her girlfriends. Sometimes they would let me in the room, and other times they would say, "You're too young—go away."

When I could, I would sit there and listen. Janice would say, "Now, what you need is confidence. Hold your head up and stick your chest out. When you walk into a room, get it into your mind that they have been waiting for you. Walk in and think, 'Here I am; now the party can start.'"

As a result of hearing these things, I'd walk into the "Y" dances with outward confidence although I was insecure inside. I had had that drilled into my head and would walk in with confidence and think, *O.K., Denice Perkins is here. Let's start the party and dance.*

After about two months of going to the "Y", I said, "Mama, my teenage life is going to pass me by. Mama, I think I want to start dating boys and not have to be head over heels in love with them. I'm going to start dating boys for just friendship."

"Denice, you should. You should just get out and date" was her reply. She wanted to see us laughing and enjoying ourselves.

The very next time I was at the "Y", one of the more popular boys at school asked me for a date. Normally I would have said no, but with my new philosophy in my brain, I said, "Sure, why not?"

He took me to an early show, and I could tell that he

was somewhat disturbed with me because I wasn't falling all over him. I was simply acting bored, which I was. After the movie we got in the car, and all he could talk about was sex and all of his conquests. I told him that I thought his bragging was "gross" and that I certainly wasn't "that type of girl."

So he simply said to me, "Well, I guess I'll take you home. There's certainly nothing further for us to do." And I agreed.

The next day at school, one of the cheerleaders came up to me and said, "Jim was talking about you last night."

I said, "What did he say?" (I certainly wanted to make sure he didn't say anything except the truth.)

"Well, he was telling everybody what a little square you were."

And I replied, "Well, that's exactly right."

Some of the other guys were there listening, and one of them said, "Well, if you're that kind of girl, I want to date you." His name was Buddy and was real good-looking. We started dating, but he simply hovered over me too much. We had gone together five dates before he even kissed me, and it wasn't long before he felt he owned me. He planned my weekends, gave me gifts, and then one day the real shocker came. He invited me to go to church with him.

I told him, "Oh, no, I can't go to church with you." He was not the same denomination that I was, and I didn't want to go to any other church than my own.

After my stepfather died, we had started going to a Methodist church near our house. That's when mom stopped taking her nerve pills. She had never wanted to take them anyway because she was afraid she would depend on them. She had also quit the psychiatrist years before because he never helped, and mom knew her help was going to be found in God although she didn't know how.

By now the Lord was also working in my life. And I had changed my opinion about Christian boys, for I had met some who were very handsome, especially one young man in the church who was not only very handsome but could also sing. Until I met him, I had thought all Christian boys wore thick glasses and braces and were just plain "turkeys."

The change in my Christian life was very gradual, nothing earthshaking. For example, one day as I was sweeping the carpet (our vacuum cleaner never worked), I noticed that I was singing Christian songs. I thought, *When did I start doing that?* And then I realized that I wasn't listening to rock music anymore. I was listening to the Christian stations and the Christian songs.

One particular day as I was sweeping away in the living room, I felt that I heard God speak to me. It was sort of like hearing myself talk. The voice said, "You're going to marry a preacher."

Immediately I started thinking about that handsome young boy in the church. And I got on the phone and called mother and said, "Mother, you'll never guess what happened! I think God spoke to me. While I was sweeping the carpet, I felt like He was telling me I was going to marry a preacher!"

Mother was so excited and said, "Denice, this is just wonderful!" And I could tell that mother was pleased that I was talking about God.

Even though Pam and Janice had gotten married, many of the guys who came around the house because of them still kept coming just to talk to mother. Her nerve problems were calming down, and she was feeling much better. We were really going through a happy stage in our lives.

One day when I went to the "Y" dance, there was a rock group playing. Everybody in the room had formed a circle, watching a guy and his girl dance. They were really good! This guy was really swift on his feet, and he had confidence in himself. Anyone could tell with one look that he thought he was the greatest gift God had ever put on the face of this earth. Yet, I kept watching because I thought he was the "toughest" thing I had ever seen in my life. My heart was beating out of time while I watched him dance.

Robin turned to me, and she said, "Denice, you think you can get any boy you want—let me see you get that guy." And she pointed to Steve.

I looked at her, laughed, and said, "Give me two weeks."

I didn't know that the girl he was dancing with had been

going with him for three years, or I wouldn't have been so brave to make that bet with her. I kept my eye on him all night, and I danced with a bunch of guys.

Then in a smart tone I said, "Robin, give me two weeks; no, better than that, I'll tell you something. That's the guy I'm going to marry."

Robin just laughed, and I laughed. But this was the first guy who had ever taken my breath away. This Steve was a challenge. Every girl in the room wanted to date him.

Steve was a college student and the manager of the rock group while I was only in the ninth grade. Then I realized he was Steve Vickers, the brother of the young boy I had kissed in the fifth grade, the boy my older sisters used to talk about.

He was leaning against a table watching the group play, and I saw his girlfriend leave and go into the bathroom. I thought, *Here's my chance.*

I walked up to him and said, "Hi, my name is Denice Perkins."

He looked at me, smiled, and said, "What do you want me to do—melt?"

I thought that was such a "smart aleck" thing to say, and it burned me up. I was used to guys saying, "Wow, yeah, how are you doing?"

I looked at him, and I knew that I had to come back with something really confident. So I said, "Well, most boys do; why shouldn't you?" He jerked his head back and laughed, and I started giggling. Just then his girlfriend walked up, and I thought, *He's not going to be interested in me.*

She was older than I, and I considered her a woman compared to me. One look, and I knew she was not an innocent little girl.

All of a sudden she grabbed both of his hands and started shaking him and saying, "Steve Vickers, I can't trust you or let you out of my sight for one second. Every time I get out of your sight, you're with another girl." The entire time she was talking, she was looking at me.

Then I looked at Steve, smiled, and said, "I think I'd better be going."

He said, "I'll see you around," and winked.

The next weekend during the evening mom let me take the car so that some of us could go out for hamburgers. Mama knew she could trust me. She knew I wasn't going to go out drinking and that I was keeping myself pure. She knew of the times I had made boys bring me home because they tried to get "fresh" with me.

We drove to Treasure Isle, a hamburger joint, to get something to eat, and I went in to buy some food. Robin and C.Y. started driving the car up and down the block, "cruising" like most of our friends. When I came back out, Robin and C.Y. hadn't come back yet.

Suddenly, someone tapped me on the shoulder. I turned around, and it was Steve! I said, "The girls that I'm with have left me; I can't find them."

"Why don't you come and sit in my car, and we can talk while you wait for them."

I thought, *This is my chance!* He had been on my mind all week.

As Steve and I sat there talking, I turned around and saw that Robin and C.Y. had returned. I turned back to Steve and said, "Excuse me while I talk to the girls."

When I got to the car, anyone would think they were going to have a heart attack. Of course, they wanted to know how this ever happened. I told them he just drove up and asked me to sit in his car. And then I told them to come back in about an hour because Steve wanted me to go for a ride with him. I had never done anything like this before, but his Cadillac was more than I could resist, let alone the boy sitting in the car.

It was apparent that Steve was certainly from a different background than mine. It was also apparent that he was used to fine things and money. So off we drove.

Steve was full of confidence, and I thought, *Boy, here's a guy who's got his stilts ready. He knows which move he's going to make next.* I was sitting there scared to death, feeling panicky in my heart because I was going for a ride at night with a guy I scarcely knew.

It wasn't long until, sure enough, he turned down a back road and headed for "the lights," an overlook where couples went to "make out." I knew that everyone would ask, "Where did you go?" And I would have to say, "We went to the lights." I had never been there before, but I'd heard all about it. You could park there and see all the lights of the city. It was a very romantic place.

My heart was almost pounding out of my chest. Steve turned the radio on (soft music of course), turned it down low, and all of a sudden I felt the seat going back and tilting. Then I remembered mama's admonition, "Never trust or go riding with a stranger."

I looked around, checking out the nearest house where I could run and use the phone. The house was a long ways away, and I sat there thinking, *Denice Perkins, you're stupid. You're going to be raped. This guy has plans.* My mind was racing.

Then I thought, *I've got to get his mind on something else.* So I jumped up and stretched out my arms, keeping him at a distance, and said, "Steve, tell me all about your girlfriend. And tell me all about yourself."

He looked at me in a funny way and said, "What do you want me to tell you that stuff for?"

Then he leaned over to kiss me on the mouth, but I was shaking so hard that he missed and kissed the end of my nose. And I thought, *You've just been raped. You've got to get out of here!*

Trying to control my panic, I looked at him and said, "I've got to go home."

And he said, "O.K." He cranked up the car and took me back to the hamburger joint, and that was it.

When I got out of the car, all he said was, "Denice, I'll see you around."

When I got into the car with C.Y. and Robin, I just looked at them like a "Cool Luke" and said, "Wow, he's really neat." They didn't know I was about ready to have a heart attack.

But in the days ahead I couldn't keep him off my mind.

Steve, at the time, was a student at the University of Alabama and was preparing to transfer to Alabama Christian College. Little did I know that Buddy and Steve were going to the same college and that they spent quite a bit of their time talking about me. Steve was giving Buddy advice on how to get me to go steady.

(from left) Pam, Janice, and I.

5.
Getting Serious

It seemed that wherever I went in town, I would see Steve. I'd go to Treasure Isle or the Putt Putt golf course or even go to fill up with gas, and there was Steve Vickers. And every time I saw him, it seemed as though he had a different girl in his car—blond, bruette, or redhead. They certainly did not look like the run-of-the-mill girls either. I just knew that Steve thought I was a real square.

One time Buddy took me to a football game, and we'd hardly gotten seated when I looked down and saw Steve Vickers. My heart started pounding.

During the game I saw Steve leave to go to the concession stand. I quickly turned to Buddy and said, "Excuse me, Buddy, but I have to go to the restroom."

"Do you want me to go with you, Denice?" he asked.

I quickly replied, "No, you just sit right here—I'll be

right back." I wanted to run into Steve.

I nonchalantly walked up to him and said, "Hi, Steve. How are ya doing?"

He turned to me and said, "Well, what are you doing?"

I said, "Oh, I'm just here with Buddy."

He looked at me for a moment, and then he said, "Well, why don't you get rid of him early, and I'll call you at home."

And I said, "That sounds like a good idea." As soon as the game was over, I told Buddy I had to get home early.

It wasn't long until Steve called me on the phone. We talked on the phone for literally hours. A couple of times before this call, he had called me at about six o'clock and said, "Hey, how about a date? I'll pick you up at six-thirty." Well, I wasn't going to let him get by with that, and I refused.

This time he asked to take me to the movies, and I thought, *I'll give this guy another try.*

When Steve picked me up for the date, he irritated me because he was so different. He acted like he was doing me the biggest favor in all the world. It was just an air he had about him. It was such an honor for him to condescend to let me get into his car when all the other boys mooned over me.

We went to the drive-in, and I noticed that he began biting his fingernails. And I thought to myself, *He's nervous about something.* After our first experience when Steve had taken me to see the lights, he hadn't tried to come on heavy anymore. Finally, Steve said to me, "Denice, Buddy is coming over to your house tomorrow afternoon to ask you to go steady with him. What's going to be your answer?"

I looked at Steve and matter-of-factly stated, "Of course it will be no. I'm not going to go steady with anybody."

"Denice, if I'd asked you, would you go steady with me?"

In my heart I was wanting to say yes. But instead I said, "Steve, I just got through telling you I'm not going steady with anybody."

We continued dating off and on from then on.

In the meantime my mother and I were continuing to go to the little Methodist church where the handsome youth pastor was assisting. One day my mother went forward in the church and was at the altar praying. I decided that I would go forward, too. As I knelt at the altar—it was after the young man had preached—I cried and cried.

The pastor came up behind me and said, "Denice, what is it you want from the Lord?"

"Oh, pastor," I responded, "I really don't know. But I need to be honest with you. I don't know whether I came down here tonight to receive a touch from God or whether I came forward because I was attracted to Mike (the youth pastor)."

The pastor laughed a little and said, "Well, thank goodness, Denice, at least you're honest." He called Mike over, and he and the pastor held my hand, and they prayed with me.

Several weeks later on my way to a "Y" dance, I stopped by the church because I saw a lot of the kids out front. I thought it would be fun just to talk and find out what was going on. My girlfriends and I pulled up, and Mike, the youth pastor, said, "Good, I'm glad you girls showed up. We need some extra help tonight on visitation."

I said, "Well, we can't do that; we're going to the dance."

At that he pointed his finger at me and said, "Denice Perkins, you dance, and you'll dance in hell." With that remark, something turned off in me. I just couldn't understand his statement. From that moment on he lost communication with me, and I lost all attraction for him.

However, my attraction for Steve grew, and I was constantly frustrated that I just wasn't woman enough for him. I looked at all the other girls that he was dating. They were so "endowed" and had such nice figures. I kept staring at myself and thinking, *Denice Perkins, you are just a prune. You're a real square.*

At one of the dances a girl came up to me and said, "You know, Denice, Steve Vickers said that you are really a cute girl and that he likes you."

Then she continued, "But you know what he said? He said, 'The only problem is that I know I can date her anytime I want to. So she's not interesting.' "

That burned me up! I knew it was the truth, and it

killed me. I went home, Robin with me, and lay across the bed and cried, "Robin, I have been such a fool. I'm a fool. I made myself a fool for that guy. He knew he could call me, and I'd run."

I got out my science notebook, and with a pencil I scratched across it, "I, Denice Perkins, will never date Steve Vickers again until I am ready." I underlined it and threw it up in the top of my closet.

Steve started calling me, and he'd say, "How about us going out tonight?"

And I'd say, "NO!" and slam the phone down.

He'd call me the next night. "How about going out tonight?"

And I'd say, "No, I'm busy." I'd hang up and bawl my eyes out.

He'd keep calling me, and I'd say, "I'm sorry. I've got other plans. I've got a date." I let the whole summer go by with him calling me and me saying no.

Finally he called and said, "Let's go out tonight."

I said, "No, I've got plans."

He said, "Let's go out tomorrow night."

And I said, "I've got plans."

He said, "Let's go out next Friday night."

And I said, "I've got plans."

He finally said, "You know, it looks like you've got plans for everybody but me."

I said, "You're exactly right; you've got it."

That really hurt his ego. So we hung up. He was hurt. Then he didn't call me at all for a long time.

About the middle of October Steve called again and asked for a date. As usual I said, "Well, I'm busy tonight. I've got a date." It wasn't long until someone knocked on the door, and I yelled, "Come in!" To my shock, there was Steve.

He looked at me and said, "I thought you were going out. You told me you had a date."

Even though I had been caught in my lie, that still didn't change my mind. Eventually Steve just left.

Sometime later Robin, C.Y., and I decided to go to the

state fair. And as we were walking along, I saw Steve again. He was part of a rock group, and they were playing. I was walking barefooted because I hated to wear shoes, and I had on black and white checked hip-huggers, with a white belt and a black shirt that laced up the front. I had seen Steve, but I was going to pretend that I didn't see him and walk right on by.

Steve came up behind me and grabbed me by the arm and said, "Do you know what you look like?" I just stood there and stared at him. "You look like a French whore. And the girl that I'm going to marry is not going to look like that."

I looked at him with my eyes flashing and said, "Well, what makes you think I'm going to marry you?"

He said, "Yes, you are." I pulled my arm back from him, and he said, "Now listen, you're going to date me tomorrow night."

I looked at him, and all of a sudden I felt, *Now, I'm ready to date him.* So I said, "O.K."

The next night he came to the door and got me. As we were driving off, he turned to me and said, "Here, hold this," and handed me a glass of wine.

When we got around the block, I turned to him and said, "Steve, take me home."

He knew I was mad. "What's this?" he said.

"I'm not going with you if you're going to drink."

He said, "O.K., O.K.," and he flung the wine, glass and all, out the window.

Then I looked him square in the eyes and said, "If you're going to date me, you're not going to drink while we're dating. You're not going to cuss, and you're going to go to church with me every Sunday."

He looked at me and moaned, "Oh, no." But from that time on, he picked me up, we'd go out, and he would be in church every Sunday. He was the attention of the church because he always looked like he stepped right out of the band box.

One Sunday morning Steve called me and said, "Listen, I'm not going to make it this morning."

That made me mad because I knew he just didn't want

to be in church. So I said, "You know, that's funny; I was fixing to call you and tell you I couldn't make it for our next date." I slammed the phone down, got dressed, and went to church.

In church I couldn't concentrate on the service because I was so mad at Steve. As I walked out after the service, the pastor said, "By the way, your boyfriend came in late. He's waiting outside for you."

Steve and I became more serious with each other, yet I never did tell Steve that I loved him—although I did. I couldn't even say to mother, "I love you." She always knew it, but I couldn't say it because I felt that if I said it, it would hurt. I felt that if I said, "I love you," I'd cry. But that was because when I was little, mother would say, "Don't touch me; it hurts." Steve would tell me how much he loved me, but I couldn't return the love.

One day Robin and I were driving around in the car, and I was wondering what kind of house Steve lived in and what his lifestyle was like. We pulled up into Treasure Isle, and I asked the girls who were sitting in the car next to us, "Do you all know Steve Vickers?"

They said, "Yeah, we know him."

I continued, "You all know where he lives?"

"Sure," they said. "Go all the way down Atlanta Highway until there are no houses, and it will be out kind of sitting by itself. It's a great big plantation home."

When we pulled up to that huge plantation house with a porch all the way across the front with huge, fat, round columns, I screamed. I was saying, "I don't believe it." Yet it looked like what he would live in.

I knew that Steve's father was a construction engineer. He looked like a Colonel Sanders—white hair, white mustache, and very dignified. He always looked like a million dollars. One look at Daddy Vickers and you knew Steve was from a fine background. His dad was a self-made man.

Steve was in the driveway washing his car for our heavy date that night. We talked to him for a minute, and then he asked us to go to the house and get some detergent. I was really scared; not only had I been taught not to call boys on the telephone, but also that a nice girl never went to a boy's home chasing him down.

We knocked on the door, and Steve's mother came to the door and said, "Come in."

So we went in, and I said, "Mrs. Vickers, Steve wanted us to come up and get some detergent." I kept thinking she was going to think I was bad because I had come to her house.

We took the detergent down to Steve, and his mother called, "Girls, come back in and we'll talk."

The house inside was like something out of *Gone With the Wind.* Robin and I sat down on the Victorian chair. We just looked at each other and felt stupid and nervous, wondering how to act. Mrs. Vickers said, "Would you all like a Coke?"

We said, "Yes."

Mrs. Vickers was a very precious woman, and when she returned with the Cokes, she really impressed this teenager. She had wrapped a napkin around each cold Coca-cola bottle before handing it to us. I thought, *Am I supposed to grab the napkin on the bottle, or am I supposed to take the bottle?* I wanted to do the proper thing, so I grabbed the napkin that was around the bottle, hoping that I had done what all dignified people do.

After Robin and I left the house, we said to each other, "Wow, do you believe that?" And I thought, *Boy have we entered class.*

Not long after that Steve and I went to church on a Sunday night, and a young man got up and sang, *Fill My Cup, Lord.* It was the first time I had heard that particular song. As he was singing it, I sat there feeling so empty—like my cup was totally empty. And I cried during the whole song.

After the service Steve and I stopped by the house and went out into the backyard as mom put the children to bed. Finally Steve asked, "Denice, why did you cry in church tonight as that boy was singing that song?"

My first reaction was to say, "Steve, I don't know," but deep inside of me I knew what was wrong. I was falling in love with Steve, and I knew he was falling in love with me. And I looked at those Christian boys, singing and preaching, and I knew that Steve wasn't a Christian yet. If I was really going to be happy, I would have to be married to a Christian. I finally looked Steve in the eye and said, "Steve, I've got to be married to a Christian. I have got to have a Christian home."

Well, to say the least, that shook Steve. He thought for a moment, and finally he said, "You know, Denice, why don't you find a guy like Mike or Gary. You need somebody like that. That's you. No way am I going to be able to be that kind of Christian. I've done a lot of wrong things and hurt a lot of girls, and, Denice, you're so innocent and pure. I don't want to spoil your life. I'm no good for you. I'm rotten through and through. I'm just going to hurt you."

(Later Steve told me that in his heart he was crying and wanting to say that he wanted to be different—if somebody could just change him. But he was afraid that he could never change. And we just left it there.)

Several days later as I was getting dressed after physical education class, a girl came up to me because she noticed a ring on my finger, and she asked, "Who are you going steady with?"

And I said, "Oh, I'm wearing Steve Vickers' ring."

She looked at me so shocked, and she said, "Steve Vickers? You're going steady with him? Well, let me tell you something about him." She proceeded to tell me of all his conquests. Other girls also tried to tell me that I couldn't be going with Steve and remain pure. They all were telling me that he didn't stick around a girl who wasn't "loose."

I just simply told them that the day he tried to touch me in the wrong way would be the day that he would get put out.

I was really very naive at the time. When some of us girls would sit around and talk, the subject seemed to always revolve around dating, petting, sex, or something of this sort. I was totally shocked and embarrassed when I heard the girls talk about all their conquests and "giving in." I thought the whole matter was very disgusting. As a matter of fact, I was so shook at some of the things they were talking about that I went home and asked my mother if some of these things were true. When my mother told me some of the facts of life, I just told her that if I ever saw a naked man, I would throw up.

However, the facts of life didn't scare me away from liking boys. Our house was still like Grand Central Station with all the kids coming by to talk to mom and drink coffee and eat homemade biscuits.

One boy named Raymond, who acted like a brother, tried to convince me to stay away from Steve and all other evils. One night I thought I would be especially adventurous. One of the girls gave me a cigarette, and I tried it and almost got sick. Raymond saw me smoking and quickly told my mother.

When I got home, my mother "beat the tar" out of me and said, "Don't you ever, ever smoke again. Don't you ever." She was crying uncontrollably. She was really disappointed in me and that hurt!

The next morning when I was getting dressed for school, she saw me in the hallway and reminded me of what I'd done. She grabbed me and started spanking me with the belt again, saying, "Don't you ever. You make me so mad. I never did pick up the habit of cigarettes. And you're not going to either." From that day on I never smoked!

Growing up, I had many responsibilities at home because mother had to work, especially after daddy left us and Bill died. It was my job to watch the two younger children and keep the house clean. We never did lock our doors, and I seemed to be so busy that Steve would get jealous of my time.

One day I came home from school and saw Steve sitting in the living room. He had cleaned the entire house. And I couldn't believe Steve Vickers would clean the house for a girl so he could talk to her. Steve was now beginning to show me that he loved me.

Another time while I was washing dishes, Steve came in looking very funny and red faced. He leaned against the door watching me wash the dishes. I said, "What's wrong with you?"

He said, "I've done something really stupid."

"What did you do?" I asked.

"Oh," he said, "it's so corny."

"Steve, what have you done?"

And he said, "Oh, Denice, I did something I never dreamed I could do." All of a sudden he pulled his hands from behind his back. There were two carnations—a red one and a white one. And as he handed them to me, he said, "I feel so dumb."

I just stared at them. I had never gotten flowers before, and I couldn't believe it. He explained, "Oh, I just went by a flower store, and I thought I'd get you something." That was so precious.

After our dates, Steve would come into our house, and we'd sit and watch television. Many nights we'd hear the national anthem and watch Channel 20 leave the air. I'd say to mama, "Tell Steve to go home. I'm tired, and I have to go to school tomorrow." He'd just sit there and laugh, and he wouldn't go home. So I'd say, "Well, I'm going to bed," and I would.

He would just stay and talk with mama. The next morning I'd wake up, and he'd be sitting in my living room, waiting for me to wake up so he could drive me to school. Within me I had to admit that I had loved him from the very night I met him. However, I still couldn't say, "I love you."

Steve would look at me, so hurt, and say, "Denice, why can't you say, 'I love you'?"

I would reply, "Steve, how many girls have you said that to, 'I love you'? It's been used so wrongly; I can't say it until it really means something." I knew I loved him, but I didn't want to say it until I knew it wouldn't hurt. I knew that "love," when I said it, would mean a total commitment.

Steve was still very much involved with the rock group, and they were really getting to the place of being recognized. People were calling them to come and play. As Christmas approached, Steve's group prepared for some important engagements, and my family and I prepared for a trip to Florida to visit my older sister. I asked Steve to come with us, and he asked me to stay home. We didn't want to have Christmas without each other.

Steve finally decided that he would go with me. This was hard for him, for he had made music his god. By doing this, I knew that this was a big step of love. He had dreamed of becoming a famous rock star. The group knew they were going to hit the big time.

When Steve went to Florida with me, that was the end of the rock band. They had been booked for Christmas and had to cancel the performance. The group fell apart.

At that time we weren't officially engaged, but Steve and I had begun talking a lot about marriage.

Steve and I went to a dance, and we weren't there long when he said, "Denice, let's go out and sit in the car and talk." As he said that, I could tell he was real nervous. When we got into the car, he looked at me and said, "Denice, I love you."

I looked at him, and all of a sudden my lips uttered the words, "Steve, I love you."

When I said that, he got so excited. "You do? You do? Really? Really?"

And I said, "Yes." It almost floored him that I could finally utter those words. I'm sure he had heard many girls say that, but I believe he knew that when I said that, it came from a heart that meant it.

"Then I have something for you," Steve said and handed me a little box. My mother had told me that Steve had bought me a charm bracelet, and when I opened the box, I expected to see the charms. Instead, I saw a diamond ring!

"No!" I gasped.

"No?" Steve quickly repeated.

"I mean yes," I uttered excitedly.

Steve and I quickly agreed to marry each other.

We went back into the dance, and I showed everybody the ring.

Then we went to my house, and Steve asked my mother, "Nellie, can I marry Denice?"

Hesitatingly, mother said, "All right, but I really should say no." Then mom seemed to go back and forth in her mind. One minute she would say yes, and the next minute she would say no. My very life seemed to hang in the balance.

Finally, she accepted the inevitable. Her sixteen-year-old daughter was going to be married.

I was sixteen years old and ready to marry Steve.

6.
Stumbling into Marriage

One day I'd wear my ring to school, and the next day I wouldn't because I wasn't sure what mom was going to end up doing. Several days later when I was in school at the drinking fountain, a girl came up to me and said, "Oh, Denice, you're engaged!"

I said, "Sure! It's to Steve Vickers!"

She quickly reacted and said, "Steve Vickers? You can't be engaged to Steve Vickers!"

"Why not?" I asked.

"Well," she said, "he's still calling this other girl all the time and talking with her on the phone."

I said, "No, he isn't."

She said, "Well, he is too."

Later I found out that Steve was simply going to the drug store and talking to a girl who was a clerk at the store.

I had to realize that Steve was just by nature a flirt. He would even flirt with the information operator on the telephone. It was just nothing, yet within me I became a little fearful of what could be a very frightening part of his life.

At any rate, now Steve and I were engaged. We were all torn up because mother wouldn't let us set a date. And now that the ring was on my finger, Steve and I really got into heavy kissing. And I knew that in the back of his mind he wanted to have sex. And if I would give any encouragement at all, I knew we would.

After several weeks we set the date for our wedding. It was February when we became engaged, and we were going to have an August wedding.

June rolled around, and I had already started taking birth control pills in preparation for the marriage.

One evening Steve and I were parked in the car kissing and hugging. On an impulse I offered myself to him.

"Denice," he said with a horrified look on his face, "I don't believe this! I never thought you would do such a thing. And I never thought that if a girl ever offered herself to me that I would say no. But, Denice, I can't touch you. I can't. And I don't even know why. I want to, but I can't."

His reaction was exciting to me, because then I knew that he really loved me. Almost everybody who knew us said that he was just wanting to use me. The ring was a ploy. But I knew differently, because now he had refused.

I went home and lay awake almost all night and kept thinking, *I offered myself to him, and he didn't accept.*

I did not realize, however, that I had let my defenses down. I should have expected what happened next.

Steve and I were out on a usual date, and before either of us hardly knew what had happened, we had had intercourse. Both of us sat there stunned, and instead of being happy or fulfilled, we were sick, depressed, and full of anguish. We were only a couple of weeks from our wedding, and we had blown it! Steve, without hardly saying a word, just started the car and began driving. All of a sudden, he pulled the car over and parked in front of the Methodist church. It was his family's church—Steve hardly went there, but his mother faithfully attended.

I looked at him and said, "Steve, what are you doing?"

He turned to me and said, "Denice, get out of the car."

As we walked up to the church, I said, "Steve, the church is locked."

He replied, "Maybe it isn't." Sure enough, Steve opened the door, and we went in.

I sat in the front pew, and as soon as I sat down, I just cried and cried. Steve went a little bit further and knelt down at the altar. He began crying and kept saying over and over and over, "God, forgive us. God, forgive us." Then he'd turn to me and say, "Denice, I'm so sorry. Denice, I'm so sorry. God, forgive us."

We were both so ashamed. We sat there for I don't know how long, just crying. We were like Adam and Eve in the garden. They had done wrong and were so ashamed.

The Lord had showed us that what we had done was sin and was wrong. We were so ashamed we felt like hiding our faces. And yet, the best we could, we apologized to God and to each other and asked for His forgiveness. Steve was so ashamed because he felt he had taken advantage of me, a virgin.

In the church I just couldn't stop crying. I had been taught all my life to stay innocent. It wasn't only because it had been drilled into me, either; it was really what I wanted. I wanted to be pure for my husband.

I looked up and saw how beautiful the church was. It had great high beams and stained glass windows. As I was looking, I saw the moon shining through the windows. Steve was still down at the altar crying, and I could see the cross. I realized that Jesus had died on that cross for such a time as this.

Steve came from the altar, and he grabbed me by the hand. He said again, perhaps for the fifteenth time, "Denice, I'm so sorry. Will you ever forgive me?"

I looked at him and said, "Steve, it was my fault too."

"No, it wasn't. It was my fault. I've been after you the whole time. I've been wanting this to happen all along." He was taking all the blame.

But after our prayer we both had a sense of total forgiveness.

The next days were filled with excitement, preparing for the wedding. Of course, mama didn't have much money, but she wanted everything to be perfect. I had responded to an ad in the paper, and I bought a beautiful gown. This was going to be a wedding to end all weddings.

A day or two before the wedding, I came home and found a letter addressed to me. It was a hate letter, obviously from a jealous girl. The letter said, "Do you think Steve has been with you every night? Where was he the other night? He was with another girl. Why don't you ask him where he was at Thursday night, and see if he'll tell you the truth?" The letter was not signed.

After I read the letter, I felt sick. I wadded it up and threw it in the trash can. Pam came to pick me up. My make-up was supposed to look good, but I had been crying. I had my wedding gown on and the veil in the box because I was supposed to have my picture taken for the paper. Pam turned to me and said, "Why don't you talk?"

"Oh, Pam, I don't want to talk."

"Denice, what's wrong with you?" she asked again.

And I said, "I don't know."

She said, "Denice, what do you mean you 'don't know'?" You don't get upset like you're upset and not know. Now, listen to me, Denice. If you're thinking of backing out, it's not too late—you still have time to do it."

I knew I couldn't tell Pam, because I wasn't going to back out. And I knew that if she knew, she would tell mother, and mother would make me back out. I went ahead and had my picture taken, came home, and then went over to Steve's house.

Steve came out and sat on the porch. I was crying. I said, "Steve, who is this girl you're seeing? Who have you been with?" And then I told him about the letter.

He lied and beat around the bush. Then he finally admitted that he had seen another girl. I was trying to push it out of my mind and cover it up. Steve's excuse was, "Denice, the reason I did it was since we are fixing to get married, I just wanted to make sure that I'm through dating girls. I took her out, and I realized that I'm really through. So I know that what I did was wrong."

To get back at Steve and cover my hurt, I said, "Well, that's all right. I'll just date this guy from Auburn who's been asking me for a date. I'll see if I'm done dating, too."

Very much to my surprise, that same guy called me up a little while later and asked me for a date. I was still so hurt that I said to him, "Yeah, I'll go out with you."

I told Steve that I was going.

My date and I went to Jasmine Hills where there are beautiful flowers and a wishing well. We stood at the wishing well, and he gave me a coin and said, "Here, make a wish and throw it in."

I made a wish that everything would work out for Steve and me. I didn't say it out loud.

Then my date said, "You want to know what I wished?"

"What was it?" I asked.

"I wished that things would work out for you and me and we'd start dating." Then he leaned over and kissed me.

I looked at him and said, "No, I love Steve Vickers. I want you to take me home."

As soon as I got home, I drove over to Steve's. He came outside in his pajamas; he was literally sick because I was with another guy.

All of the misery that my mother had been through was now coming to my mind. I was totally convinced that all men were bad; they were all women chasers, and if I were to be married to one, his antics would be part of the marriage. The wedding was going to make no difference. Steve would always play around. But I loved him so much that I was fully prepared to marry him anyway.

The day of my wedding I was determined that this was going to be my day. Daddy was going to give me away, and I asked him if he and mom would please, even though they were divorced, act like friends and not fight.

I was scared to death, as I suppose all brides are. There were over 600 guests, along with eight bridesmaids, eight groomsmen, a maid of honor, a best man, a flower girl, and the ring bearer. The church was filled to capacity.

After we had said our vows, the pastor turned us toward the large congregation and said, "Ladies and gentlemen, I would now like to introduce to you Mr. and Mrs. Steve Vickers." Steve was twenty, and I was still sixteen.

I was so relieved it was over that I gave out a great big sigh. When I did, all the people in the audience started laughing.

When we got to the foyer of the church, Steve and I were so happy we were crying and hugging all the bridesmaids and groomsmen. Steve grabbed me and flung me around in a circle, my dress flying in the air. Pam and Janice were two of the bridesmaids, my sister Lee Ann was the flower girl, and my little brother Charlie was the ring bearer.

As Steve was spinning me around in the foyer only minutes after the wedding, I began to hear a voice in my head. It was saying, *Denice, don't be a fool. You know there's no such thing as a good marriage. You know this isn't going to work out.* And even in the reception line, I kept thinking, *This will never work. You know there isn't such a thing as a good marriage.*

Then I thought, *I don't care if it doesn't work out—as long as I can be married to him for just a little while.* I loved Steve so much that I thought it would be enough just to share a little of his life.

And then suddenly it was like the devil himself was screaming at me, saying, "He's going to hurt you."

And my mind would scream back, *I don't care! I'm still going to be married to Steve Vickers.*

To make matters worse, while we were in the reception line, one of the bridesmaids' mothers leaned over and whispered in my ear, "Denice, you're far too young to get married. But I guess it's too late to say anything to you now." Satan really seemed to be working against me.

We had an evening wedding, and after the reception we headed out of Montgomery to the hotel where we had reserved a honeymoon suite. I was really scared and nervous about Steve seeing me with no clothes on. I suppose many brides go through this. He could tell I was nervous, so he said,

"Why don't we stop and get something to eat." We went into a nice restaurant and ordered some steak. The candles were burning, and it was rather dark. Our car had been all painted up and decorated with cans and the typical wedding paraphernalia, and the waitress came up to us and turned to me and asked, "Are you the ones with the car outside?"

And I said, "Why, yes, we just got married."

She said, "Listen, honey, you've got to get a divorce. You have got to get it annulled immediately."

We both looked at her and couldn't believe what we were hearing—and especially that she would have the gall to say this on our wedding night.

"Why are you saying this?" I asked.

And she answered, "I just read the charts in my horoscope, and I knew that you would be coming in and that I was to tell you that you had to get your wedding annulled before it was too late."

Her words made me nervous, and the pit of my stomach ached. I kept telling myself, *I won't receive that horoscope business. That's of the devil, and we're Christians.* But I didn't know exactly what to do. I was a Christian but had not learned how to make Christ the Lord of my life so that such things could not harm me.

The incident with the waitress put a cloud over our wedding night. Finally, we simply tried to shrug it off by saying, "Aw, that waitress is nuts."

We left the restaurant and went to our honeymoon suite. I was getting the typical new bride jitters. Steve said, "Baby, why don't you go put on your nightgown, and I'll get us some champagne."

I thought to myself, *I don't even know if I like champagne. I've never tasted it.* But I reasoned, *Well, maybe it will help me relax so that I won't be so shocked.*

I retired to the bathroom, and I thought to myself, *I've got to put on this nightgown, but I certainly don't want to take my bra off.* And I debated, *Should I? Shouldn't I? Should I? Shouldn't I?* Finally, I thought, *Well, I'll take it off. Steve will never forgive me if I'm this stupid on my wedding night.*

I opened the door a crack, and Steve was standing there in his pajama bottoms. I thought, *Oh, I can't go out into that room.* I cracked the door a little wider and saw the bed. I thought to myself, *I'll just make a run for it.*

And so, without any further hesitation, I threw open the door, and before Steve realized what was happening, I jumped in bed, grabbed the two pillows, and covered myself. And there I sat.

He looked at me thinking, *What is this silly girl doing?* I really felt dumb, but everything worked out just the way honeymoons always do.

Our honeymoon lasted for five days, and we came home to a little house we had rented on the Atlanta Highway. It was a perfect little honeymoon cottage. Steve's parents had given us bedroom furniture, living room furniture, a dining room set, a washer and dryer—everything that two kids could hope for. They had been so kind and sweet to us.

From our wedding we had received every gift we could possibly have hoped for. On the surface everything looked like our marriage was off to a good start. But my own insecure background and Satan's subtle ways were soon to be roadblocks in my quest for happiness.

7.
Suspicions

Steve and I quickly settled into married life. He had a job in a department store and was making about $100 a week. We thought that was a lot of money, and we got along very nicely on it. We paid only forty-seven dollars a month for our rented home, and that included utilities.

I was still in school, wanting to finish the eleventh grade. Steve was in the U.S. Naval Reserve, which meant that every Monday night he had to attend the reserves meeting.

I had only bad experiences on which to pattern my marriage, and I began acting just like my mother had acted. I never had had a deep trust for Steve, and I quickly became suspicious of him.

I became a sixteen-year-old detective, trying to find clues to prove Steve was not faithful to me. I would look in his shirts for the telltale thread and examine his collars for any sign of makeup. I was constantly imagining that Steve was out with another girl.

I was immature and suspicious, and I let my mind run wild about what Steve was doing. I had no peace of mind and did not know how to get the peace I needed.

Pretty soon things began to happen which started confirming my suspicions about my marriage partner.

Steve worked in the camera department of the department store, and every time I went to see him, it seemed that he was always talking to a girl from another department. She had long black hair, false eyelashes, and was extremely attractive.

One day I walked in while she was at the camera department looking at pictures. Trying to be nice, I said to her, "Oh, did you get some pictures?"

She said, "Yeah, you want to see them?" They were pictures of her posing and trying to be real sexy.

"These are really good shots," I said. "Who took these for you?"

She said, "Oh, the man that works here in the camera department, Steve Vickers."

"How nice of him," I replied. "I'm his wife."

"Didn't Steve tell you about his spending the day with me taking the pictures?" she asked.

"He probably did. I've just forgotten," I answered. But I knew he hadn't.

I became increasingly jealous and didn't want to let Steve out of my sight.

Steve's day off was Tuesday, and I would usually try to stay home from school if I could. But I couldn't do it very often because the school began complaining about my absenteeism.

I was almost insanely jealous over Steve and watched every move he made. One night I was sitting at home while he was at a reserves meeting. My mind was imagining all sorts of things, and I just couldn't stand it any longer. I borrowed mother's car, got in, and went to see if Steve was indeed at the reserves meeting. I drove to see if I could find him, and by the time I got there, I was so beaten down with fear that I was getting sick.

There was a little hotel across from where the naval reserves met, and I saw a car that looked like ours. I ransacked the whole car, not even sure that it was our car, looking for evidence. I then returned home and sat there, waiting for him to come. When he came in, I asked him, "How was the meeting?"

He said, "Oh, the same old stuff."

But I was sitting there thinking, *Yeah, I went through our car. It was parked in front of the hotel, wasn't it?* I didn't want to ask him because I was frightened. I knew much of it was simply a figment of my imagination that I had allowed to creep into my mind.

It wasn't long after that until Steve had to go away for two weeks of summer camp. The day after he left, I was sitting in the living room and was absolutely hysterical. Steve's mother came over and said, "Denice, what's wrong?"

I said, "Mrs. Vickers, I can't stand it." Steve had only been gone a day, but here I was half crazy.

Trying to comfort me, his mother said, "Denice, a lot of women's husbands go off to war, and they're gone a long time. And one of these days Steve might be gone a long time. Then what are you going to do?"

"Oh, Mrs. Vickers, I just can't help it. I can't stand him being away." She thought I was just lonesome, but really I was in torment thinking he and the guys were out drinking with women. The whole time he was gone I was almost in a state of panic.

One day Steve was called into active duty and received his orders to go to the Great Lakes Naval Training Station in Illinois. I decided that I was going to go with him.

The night before we were to leave, there was a party given. Of course, everyone was drinking and dancing with everybody else's wife. I wasn't about to have any part of that. Men would come up to me and ask me for a dance, and I would say, "No, thank you." I had no desire to be with anyone but Steve.

But in the meantime Steve was dancing with all the women who were there. Then he'd come to me and say,

"Denice, I don't want to, but I've got to be nice." I knew deep inside, however, that he wanted to.

One particular woman, Jane Doe, looked like a real "tramp." She was in her late twenties or early thirties and kept looking at Steve. I could tell she thought of me as a seventeen-year-old *kid* he was married to.

Steve had been drinking pretty heavily and was dancing and having the time of his life. This one woman said, "Oh, Denice, you're so sweet," trying to make me feel like a little girl.

And then they began to gibe me about not drinking or dancing. They could easily see how jealous I was. Jane came over to me and said, "How long have you been married, Denice?"

I said, "A year."

She said, "Have you gotten the itch to flirt yet?"

"Well, of course not. I never will," I replied.

Then she said, "You just wait 'til the seventh year. Then you'll get the seven year itch, and you'll get it bad. And your husband will start running around then, believe me."

I looked at her angrily and said, "Steve and I will never run around. We're in love."

Then I noticed her looking at Steve very strangely. I turned him around and asked, "Why is that girl looking at you like that?"

He looked at me sheepishly and said, "I don't know. She's just a tramp." But I knew all along he saw her for what she was. And I knew what he was thinking.

The next morning as we were packing up, I was still so jealous over the night before that I decided to do a little detective work. I got Steve's wallet and went through it. And sure enough, I found a slip of paper with a phone number pencilled on it.

I wonder what this is? In my mind I kept thinking, *Oh, don't worry. No big deal.* But I had to find out. My curiosity got the best of me.

I dialed the number, and I asked, "Who's speaking please?"

The girl answered, "Jane Doe." It was that girl, that

tramp, who had been making a play for him! I slammed the phone down and went to Steve. I showed him the paper. That was my green thread just like mother's. I said, "Look at this! Look at this! I've got the goods on you. Steve Vickers, what have you got to say about this?"

Then Steve replied with his big song and dance routine to cover up his lies, saying, "Well, she was just being nice and said that if we ever came back this way that I should visit her or give her a call. And she handed me her phone number."

I became violent, threatening to go out into the living room and tell his parents what I had just discovered. I wanted to tell them that their son had the phone number of a tramp. Steve started pushing me and shoving me around, saying, "Quiet, Denice. You shut up! I don't want my parents to know."

I felt so insecure in the marriage anyway. I had a false feeling that his parents hadn't wanted me to marry Steve. I felt that I had to get the goods on him.

Steve's mother heard us arguing. She came in—such a precious peacemaker. She wanted everybody to be happy. That is just the type of person she was. But I had already settled it in my mind—Steve had the phone number; he was having an affair with her, and that settled it.

When he went into the other room, I marched straight for the telephone, dialed the number, and got Jane Doe on the other end. And I said, "Jane?"

And she answered, "Yes."

I said, "This is Denice Vickers; you know, Steve Vickers' wife?"

"Oh, yes. Hello, Denice."

Then I made up a story and said, "Steve's told me all about you. He gave me your phone number and was laughing the whole time he was telling me because he had made such a fool out of you. Do you want to know what my husband said about you?" I continued. "He said that you have got to go with young men because you're so old and wrinkled. And the only reason you go out with young men is that you try to keep yourself young. You can't handle a man your own age. You haven't got what it takes!"

She said, "What?"

I said, "Sorry, Jane. You should be young like me, baby!" And I slammed the phone down.

After I hung up the phone, I was so mad that I looked Steve in the eyes and said, "There's no way I'm going to stay in this marriage with you! You can get yourself up to Great Lakes! I'll get the divorce papers and send them to you." I got in the car and went over to mother's.

I didn't tell mother because I knew that if I did, all the hurt she'd had from daddy those twenty years would cause her to say, "Get out of the marriage." I knew the bitterness would overcome her sense of reason, and she'd be almost ready to kill Steve. She'd feel what I was feeling because she still wasn't healed of all her hurts.

I didn't want to tell her what was wrong. I just said, "I'm gonna spend the night with you tonight." I asked, "Listen, may I use your car? I want to run somewhere."

She said, "Sure, Denice, you can use it."

I got in the car and was going to go and talk with the pastor of the little Methodist church that I was attending. I was going to tell him what had happened and ask him for help.

I got in the car and didn't realize how fast I was going. I was driving and crying the whole time I was trying to get to the pastor's house.

All of a sudden I saw a blue light flashing behind me. I pulled over to the side, rolled down the window, and watched a policeman walk toward me. At that moment I was mad at everybody—I was mad at my dad, I was mad at Steve, I was mad at Steve's dad, every man that ever lived, and I was mad at me.

Then the policeman came up to the window and said, "Lady, where's the fire?"

I retorted, "What's your problem?"

He backed up and looked at me. Then he said, "Listen to me!"

I replied, "Listen to *me*. I don't like my husband, I don't like my father, and I don't like you. So don't bother me." I rolled up the window and was fixing to drive off.

He tapped on the window, and I rolled it down. He asked me again, "Lady, what's your problem?"

I said, "I just found a phone number in my husband's wallet. So listen to me. If you don't want trouble, don't bother me. Let me drive. Let me alone."

He looked at me, and because he was compassionate, he said, "O.K. ma'am. Just don't kill yourself. And tell me, where are you going?"

"I'm on my way to my pastor's house," I replied.

"O.K. But drive slowly."

I rolled up the window and sat there and cried. The only reason I had wanted to tell the policeman off was because he was another man coming to drive me crazy.

I drove to the pastor's home, but he wasn't there. So I went to see a little lady who attended the church and talked with her. She tried to help me, but nothing brought me peace.

Finally I returned to mother's house. I was thinking, *O.K. You don't know for a fact that he was with this girl. You don't have the proof; all you have is the phone number.* So I thought, *You're moving hundreds of miles away. You can start over because you still don't have the proof.*

I went over to Steve's parents' house, and Steve's dad came out on the porch. I guess he was mad at me, and he certainly had the right to be. He said, "What do you want?"

And I said, "I want to talk to my husband."

He surprised me by saying, "Listen, why don't you go home and leave Steve alone."

With some emotion I said, "I want to talk to Steve."

He wasn't going to tell Steve that I was outside. He continued, "Denice, do you know what your problem is? You're a religious nut. All you talk about is God and the Bible."

I went into the house and saw Steve's mother cooking the meal. I went into the bedroom, looking for him, and there he was on his knees praying. Here he was, not even a Christian, but he had been praying and asking God to please send me back.

When I saw him praying, I thought to myself, *Thank*

you, Lord. He really wants this marriage to work.

We got back together, loaded up the truck, and took off for Great Lakes.

When we got to Great Lakes and got settled in our little apartment, we started hunting for a church to go to. We picked a little Methodist church because it was closest to our apartment. At that time we really didn't care which church we went to. We just knew that the Baptists immerse and the Methodists sprinkle. There really wasn't too much difference. We thought that if you believed in God, you were a Christian. We had never heard of an "anointing" or that one pastor could preach or teach better than another. We thought going to church was all we needed to do.

Both Steve and I had gone to the altar many times, but then that was just the thing all the kids were doing. And it is strange, but as I look back now, I never heard anyone talking about finding Jesus or having a personal experience with Him.

It wasn't long until I was teaching a little kids' class on Wednesday nights. Steve, of course, said, "I'm not going to church on Wednesday nights." Again I became suspicious.

We lived next door to two girls who were very "loose." Consequently, Wednesday night I had to force myself to go to church. And every time I would get about fifty feet from the apartment, Satan would start putting all sorts of things into my mind.

I remember one night in particular a voice seemed to say to me, "Play a trick on him. Make him think you're going to go to church, and then drive back real quietly, and you'll catch him in that girl's apartment. You'll catch him in the act."

I'd say, "No, I'm going to church. I'm going to do what's right." Yet it was almost impossible for me to keep my mind enough to teach.

While we were at Great Lakes, we discovered a friend of ours from Montgomery. His name was Ken McNiel. Ken was getting ready to get married and bring his wife Stacy to live on the base.

We all became very close since we were from the same hometown. Stacy was a beautiful girl with frosted hair, long eyelashes, and long fingernails. If Stacy was going to take garbage out, she'd take her curlers out before she took it out, even though she needed to roll it again as soon as she got back into the house.

We'd go bowling, shoot pool, go to the club on the base, and do all sorts of things together. They'd drink, and I'd sip on my Coke. Everyone would tease me about sipping my Coke and would say, "You'll grow up one of these days and be able to drink."

I'd see Ken and Stacy enjoying each other, and I'd think, *Steve and I are two different people, where Stacy and Ken are one.* Yet Steve never wanted me to "come down" to their level.

I knew somehow that in God there had to be an answer. So I began my search in a local Christian bookstore, really thinking that I would find an answer in some book. I'd buy any book I saw that had a title which seemed to match one of my problems. It could be on happiness, success, how to be a total woman, or whatever. Many times I would go in and buy six or seven books at one time. I would read and read, even on my lunch hour.

By this time both Stacy and I had gotten a job at a nearby department store. I embarrassed her by reading so much. As a matter of fact, she would ask me to cover up the book so no one would know the type of material I was reading.

One day a couple of her friends were to join us for lunch, and she asked that I not bring my Bible or books and read in front of them because they would think I was crazy.

I promised her that I would play it straight and not mention God or bring a book or anything. She had no way of knowing how deeply her remarks had hurt me as I desperately searched for something that would give me peace in our marriage.

Our going out became even more frequent, and the drinking increased. I really didn't want to go, but I was afraid to let Steve go by himself. And so to save the ridicule, I started taking drinks. I had listened to Satan's lie, "If you don't join 'em, you'll lose 'em."

Even then Steve didn't like what I was doing because he

was holding me up on a pedestal—the pure, innocent Denice. He hadn't wanted me to take a drink. He had been proud that I sat at the table and sipped my Coke. He had wanted me to stay clean. But he didn't require any of that purity for himself.

The fear within me was so strong that I really felt that Steve wanted a different kind of girl. Having never drunk in my life, one mixed drink would make me totally drunk.

One night as the band was playing, I got up in front of everybody and started doing some kind of a flimsy strip act. Steve came and tried to get me to stop. Inside me I was saying, *I'll show him. I'll show him I can be like one of those tramps he likes!* Then the other half of me would look at him and plead, *Steve, see what you're doing to me? See what you're doing to me?* I was in such a battle that I thought I would lose my sanity.

I only acted this way a few times because I couldn't stand the taste of beer, and margaritas tasted like pure salt water. I just hated all of it. But I knew deep within that I had to show him.

When we got home that night, I was drunk. Steve looked at me and said, "Denice, you're so good and sweet and pure. Please don't ever do that again. Please promise me you'll never do that again." He wanted a pure wife, but he wanted to play around and live in his own low standards. I had found out that my taking on his standards would never be an answer.

The following Sunday I went to church by myself because Steve just wouldn't get out of bed. After the service the pastor stood at the door shaking everyone's hands, and as I walked by, he grabbed my hand and said, "We're so glad to have you with us this morning."

I looked at him and started crying. I cried, "Please help me! Help me! Please help me! Pastor, please help me!" I was searching for just one person who would stand up and say, "I have the answer; this is what you've got to do."

But the pastor of that church didn't know what to do. He patted me on the back and said, "Come back and visit us again," and he pushed me through the crowd. He added as he pushed, "Now you come back and see us again, dear."

I got into the car in the parking lot and sat there, crying and screaming, "God, where are You? God, God, what about me? What about me, Denice Vickers? God, are You there? Do You care? Do You have an answer for my life? I don't care what You've done in everybody else's life. God, You've got to do something in my life! God, I'm so tired of searching for You and never finding You, and if You're really here, You'd better show me because I'm tired of this playing around. You'd better get busy!" That might not be a very spiritual attitude, but that's exactly the way I felt. I got myself together and went home. Again I was the sweet, good little Denice for the rest of the day, with Steve not knowing that inside I was a dying wife.

Several days later Stacy and I decided that we were going to surprise our husbands and have lunch with them. I didn't like Steve to drink, and when it became such a problem, I had asked him not to. He had promised me he wouldn't. So naturally I thought he was keeping that promise. I didn't want any liquor in the house.

Despite the confusion and turmoil in my own mind, I was trying to convert Steve, trying to clean up his act, trying to change him. I didn't realize that I couldn't change him or anyone else; only God could change my husband. About the only thing I accomplished was to make him so bitter that he resorted to lies and began doing things behind my back.

When we drove up, I saw Steve "cutting up" with a bunch of his friends. He had been drinking to such an extent that he went over to a fire hydrant and lifted his leg, pretending that he was a dog. I got out of the car and walked up to him. I could smell the liquor all over him. Normally Steve was always glad to see me and was sweet to me. But suddenly he looked at me with hate in his eyes and asked, "What are you doing here?"

At that point we had a "wing-ding" fight. Finally, I angrily got into the car, and Stacy and I drove off.

Suddenly Stacy looked at me and said, "I want to tell you something. You've got a problem." And she continued, "Your problem is that you love your husband too much. You take life too seriously." Then she said encouragingly, "Why don't you enjoy yourself? Have some fun."

I started crying and said, "Stacy, I can't. I just can't."

"Yes, you can," she replied. And she began to name all the fun things she had done before she got married—such as getting drunk and going with many men—and she said, "You haven't lived. You don't know what it's like to live."

"Stacy, I can't. Don't you understand me when I say I can't? I'm a Christian, and I can't do those things. There is something missing in my life. I know it's not liquor and all those things you just told me about. One of these days I'm going to find out what it is. Stacy, I believe it is going to be found in God. God has something to give me, but I don't know yet how to receive it."

The time passed at Great Lakes, and our husbands graduated and prepared to go away on a cruise. Stacy, who was complaining about arthritis, and I decided we would go back to Montgomery and leave Ken and Steve at Great Lakes.

After we arrived back in Montgomery, Stacy's ailment was diagnosed as bursitis, and I continued to be tormented with my own kind of pain. I kept dreading and fearing what my husband was doing up there at Great Lakes. He, after all, had the perfect set-up—his own apartment and no wife to watch him.

Once when I called him, he sounded so strange. I could hear guilt in his voice. He said he and some others were playing cards, but I knew he was lying. Truth and suspicion were co-mingled in my mind, and I didn't know what was fact and what wasn't. I realize now that Satan was trying to destroy me and my marriage, but back then I couldn't tell what was truth and what was Satan's lies.

Our first year of marriage was drawing to a close, and it had often been a stormy adventure. But as our first anniversary approached, I became excited and wanted it to be exciting and romantic. I anxiously waited for Steve to come home so that we could share some married "bliss."

When Steve came home for our first anniversary, he brought a surprise with him—a sailor buddy! Not only that, he brought the other sailor's laundry too. He asked me to take all the white uniforms and launder them. Of course, that required starching and ironing them also.

I ended up spending my entire anniversary day washing and starching and ironing uniforms. The more I worked, the more angry I became.

By the time they walked in the door, I was so mad I was ready to throw the iron at them. When he came through the door, I started slinging clothes and what-have-you at him.

Suddenly he threw me a wrapped package and said, "Well, here then." What he had actually been doing was shopping to buy me a gift. It was a beautiful, sheer, black negligee.

We quite obviously tried to regain our composure. The other sailor knew it was no place for him, so he returned to the base. We went out and got a hamburger and came home to eat it. Suddenly, Steve took his fist and hit the hamburger. The insides went flying all over the place. Steve was sitting there in a pair of shorts, and I took the bismark that I had been eating and smashed it, jelly and all, against his bare leg. At that point we stared at each other and just started laughing.

The tension between us was broken, and it seemed that the storm clouds had parted and we were once again in the sunshine. I didn't realize that this might only be the eye of the storm where all is calm and that the storm could pick up in intensity at any moment.

8.
Moving and Searching

Steve was now stationed at Norfolk, Virginia, and returned there to be shipped out. However, when he got to the base, he discovered that he would not be shipped out for two months, and I decided to go to Norfolk to stay with my sister, who happened to live there, so that I could be close to him.

Steve's ship finally left Norfolk and docked in Boston. Naturally, being the loyal (and suspicious) wife that I was, I drove up to Boston to be with him for the four months he was to be there.

As I travelled to Boston, I couldn't help but think of the mess our marriage was in. I realized that Satan was making my mind think absurd things. I told myself that I was really a nut and such a "klutz" for putting up with Steve because I had caught him in lie after lie. Here I was making the sacrifice to go to Boston when I knew good and well that I should simply pack up and leave him.

I had never driven in big cities; nor did I know how to read a map, but I wasn't scared. I was determined to see Steve. Mom expressed concern about me going alone that far, but she said she knew God would take care of me.

All during this time, the songs my mother had taught me began to come to me. I would drive down the freeway, singing all the songs that I had sung as a little girl. Both the songs and the Scripture my mother had taught me when I was little were now helping me keep my sanity. Almost every morning of my early life mother, despite her personal torment, would say to me, "Denice, never forget God. God is the answer." Now I kept clinging to that belief although I didn't know how God would do things.

I kept singing over and over again, "I Know the Lord Will Make a Way for Me." Somewhere in the song was the thought that if I lived a holy life and shunned the wrong and did the right, the Lord would make a way for me. Yet, I really didn't know how to shun wrong or what to do. I was so confused.

As I approached what I thought was Boston—I couldn't read a map—I stopped the car and rolled down the window. I called out to a man who was driving beside me and asked, "Sir, could you please tell me where I am?"

He said, "Ma'am, you're in New York City."

I said, "Oh, I figured that because all the buildings are so big." I began to realize how simple it was just to follow the lines on the map.

When I got into Boston, just to make sure I was there, I stopped at a service station and said to the man, "Am I in Boston?"

The man replied, "Yes, ma'am, that's where you're at!" So I asked him if I could use his bathroom. I was in blue jeans and a sweatshirt and had curlers in my hair and didn't have any make-up on. I wanted to fix up. Before going to the bathroom, I went to the phone and called Steve. I was so glad to hear his voice. Steve was excited. He told me to stay there, and he would get someone to drive him over to the station.

So I went into the bathroom and got dressed with stockings, high heels, and the whole business. I really wanted to look sharp for Steve.

When I walked out, the gas station attendant said, "Are you the woman who went in there with those curlers, and you're coming out looking like this?" That kind of thrilled me because I thought I would look that nice to Steve also.

Steve and I had a sweet reunion and immediately went looking for an apartment. Because our income was so limited, we knew that we'd have to get an apartment almost next to skid row. Even though we had so many problems, I knew down deep that Steve loved and cherished me. And I knew it bothered him that he couldn't always give me the very best.

On the front door of the apartment we rented someone had scrawled out, "Beware of Rats." I thought it was a joke, but to my horror it was the truth. There was a long, dark hallway with all the doors open to the various apartments. Everybody stood their trash out by the door, and it was the most shocking thing I had ever seen in my life. I was scared to death. It was all I could do just to open up the door of my apartment and come out.

We were really in a tough neighborhood. The girl next door was a prostitute and using her apartment for her labors. That hit me head on, and I just knew that Steve would be paying her a visit.

We rented some furniture, and I tried my best to make the apartment look liveable. But try as I would, I couldn't do it. We had no lamp, and there was no ceiling light, so our TV was our only form of light. We used the bed as our table on which to eat. Lima beans, eggs, and bread were practically all we ate during the months I was in Boston. When I went to buy grits, everyone just laughed at me. I finally went out and got a job, which helped us survive.

The curtains were so filthy that after Steve had left for the ship one morning, I thought I would walk over to the laundromat and try to wash them. I had no more gotten the clothes into the washing machine when a man walked in. I was rummaging through my purse, looking for some change, and I looked over and noticed he was washing his hair in the sink. I thought, *What is going on?*

Then I thought, *Well, he must work here,* because he didn't seem to be paying any attention to me. I turned around and asked, "Sir, could you give me change for a dollar bill?"

And he said, "Sure."

When I pulled the dollar out of my purse, I looked at him, and his pants were down! Quickly I thought, *I've got to keep my composure.* So I grabbed my purse, which was sort of a throw bag, and said to him, "You come near me, and I'll kill you!" I said it very firmly and sounded mean. And he must have believed me, for he jerked his trousers up and ran out the door. I ran out the door right behind him.

Then when it hit me, I was afraid to go home. I knew he would follow me back. I was also afraid to go back and get my curtains because I thought he'd come in and corner me.

Just then a real old lady walked in. I thought, *I guess I'll go in there and check on my curtains.* I turned to the lady and said, "You'll never believe what happened to me just now."

And when I finished telling her, she said, "That's funny. I know the guy you're talking about. He comes in every morning and washes his hair in the sink. He's never done that to me." I kind of chuckled, because she had to be eighty.

When I opened up the washing machine, all that was left of the curtains had totally fallen apart. All I had was a pile of strings.

Steve and I tried to settle in a church in Boston, but we never seemed to find one to fit. We watched television a lot, and one night Steve and I watched Billy Graham together. As Billy Graham gave the altar call, I glanced over at Steve and saw tears flowing down his face.

That touched me deeply, yet the next day Steve was the same old Steve. He wanted to be different; he hated the way he was. But Satan had him bound, and he could not change—not even for me. At the time neither he nor I knew that it was Satan. I simply didn't think Steve could change.

After our stay in Boston, we moved to Jacksonville, Florida. I got a job with the bank while Steve remained on the ship. Steve told me they were going to go on a small cruise. And because his brother was getting married the next weekend, I decided that I would drive from Jacksonville to Montgomery and attend the wedding.

Coming back, I saw signs along the road, saying "Madame Christine—she'll tell you your future and your fortune." I was searching for God or for anybody who could give me an answer. *I wonder how much it would cost?* I thought and decided I would go in and see what she had to say. I took my rings off so that she wouldn't know I was married, put them in my purse, and pulled up to her house.

As soon as I met her, I asked her the dumbest question. I don't know what I was expecting her answer to be, but I said, "First of all, before I do this, I want to ask you something. Madame Christine, are you a Christian?"

She answered me, "Well, yes, my dear, don't you see that I have a picture of Jesus right over there on the wall?"

And I said, "O.K." When I sat down, I felt guilty because I had taken my ring off. So I said, "I've got to tell you, I'm married." And I put my ring on because I didn't want to be deceitful.

Then she started telling my fortune. She said, "I see that you're going to have three children." Then she continued by saying, "You'll have two boys and a girl." Then with amazement and a horrified look on her face, she told me that there were lies going on about me right then. "There are a brunette and a blond telling lies about you, and it is getting to your husband."

I thought to myself, *This can't be true because I don't know anybody in Jacksonville who could be telling a lie about me.*

She continued, "There is going to be a man coming into your life. He has black, wavy hair and green eyes. He's six feet tall."

As she continued, I thought, *Oh, this is crazy. What am I doing here?*

Then she said to me, "Your husband has something to do with construction, doesn't he?"

I replied, "Yes . . . well, after he gets out of the navy, he's going to be in construction."

Then she said, "I see a separation. I see your husband going away for a long time." Then she told me a few other trivia things that didn't seem to matter.

I left there and still felt empty and without any answers. At the time I couldn't place anybody in Jacksonville who was brunette or blond.

Shortly after that I received a letter from Steve, bawling me out and saying he couldn't believe what Barry had been telling him. Barry had received a letter from his wife saying that I had let a guy on the beach talk dirty to me. His letter was really telling me off. Then all of a sudden it hit me—Barry was brunette, and his wife was a blond.

What had actually happened was that a man had come up to me while I was on the beach and had asked me out. I said, "No, I'm married," and got up and went into the water to try to get him to leave me alone. Barry's wife Miriam had been lying next to me on the beach, and she observed the entire episode.

The night after I received the accusing letter, Miriam came over, and I showed her the letter and said, "Now, tell me when this guy talked dirty to me."

She said, "Well, Denice, you didn't hear it. Remember when you went down to the water?"

I said, "Yeah."

"Well, this guy came up to me and told me what he'd like to do to you."

I said, "I didn't hear it."

Miriam replied, "Well, I forgot to tell you."

And then I remembered, *That's the lie that the fortune teller was telling me about.* And I was terrified because deep down I knew that fortune tellers had to be from Satan and that I had been wrong to go to her.

A couple of days later I answered a knock on the door and couldn't believe my eyes when I opened the door. There was the same man, tall with black wavy hair and green eyes. He looked at me and said, "I've seen you walking around the block. I pinpointed that you lived here, and I wondered if you'd like to go out?"

I said, "No thank you, I'm married."

"Aw, come on," he pleaded. "You know your husband is out to sea."

I said, "Yes, he is."

"Well, come on then. Let me take you out to eat. It won't do any harm."

I firmly responded, "No. I'm married. You don't understand. I'm a born again Christian."

He said, "Well, come on. You don't think for a minute that your husband is true to you! I was in the navy, and, let me tell you, when they pull into port, he's going to have some fun. So, girl, it isn't going to hurt for you to come out and have some fun with me."

I stood my ground and replied, "Look, mister, even if my husband does those things, I'm a Christian and I can't."

He stood there, and all of a sudden he started to cry and said, "I never dreamed I'd see a woman who would say no."

"Well, you've met one," I replied. We continued talking, and he began to tell me about his wife and how messed up their marriage was. It frightened me how that fortune teller was getting things right.

Then Steve came home and said his ship was pulling out and would be gone for nine months. I thought, "Now here's the separation she told me about."

Just before Steve got word that he would be gone for nine months, I had gone to the doctor because I thought I was pregnant. He couldn't tell for sure and asked me to come back in a couple of weeks. In the meantime, Steve had taken me home to Montgomery, where I had made arrangements to move in with mama for the time Steve would be gone on the cruise.

When Steve had returned and gone to sea, and as soon as I was settled, I discovered for sure from the doctor on the base that I was pregnant. I wrote Steve and told him that we were "expecting."

Mama was so glad to have an adult in the home with whom she could talk and share her problems. Soon after I came home, mother came to me and said, "Denice, I have a wonderful idea for us while you're here for these nine months. Why don't we spend this time really searching for more of God."

I looked at her and screeched, "Mama, this is just what I want! I know this is what I need in my life."

While drinking coffee, we looked at each other and talked. Mama said, "You know, Denice, we're born again Baptists."

And I said, "Yeah, I know mama."

She continued, "We're attending the Methodist church, but I believe for some reason that we shouldn't think of a church or denomination if we're really going to find God. We've got to search for Him, and not necessarily a certain denomination."

We started visiting churches and were quite amazed at how some handled sin so lightly. At one church we attended, the pastor came to the platform and said, "Before we start the service, I'd like to make an announcement. I've noticed that between Sunday school and church that a lot of board members and Sunday school teachers have been smoking in front of the church. I would like to request that you men please smoke your cigarettes on the side of the church because it doesn't look good to the people passing by. Besides that, we don't like sweeping up the cigarette butts."

Mother and I looked at each other. I said, "Mama, if it's wrong to smoke in front of the church, why isn't it wrong to smoke beside the church?" So we decided right then and there that this minister couldn't teach us how to find a deeper experience with God.

Mother and I continued to spend most of our time going from church to church, but we found little or nothing.

As the time approached for Steve to come home, mother said, "Denice, we must visit Evangel Temple. Everyone is saying that something is happening there."

I said, "Oh, mama, what could be happening in a church?" I just couldn't imagine that anything exciting could happen in a church.

Mother said, "Well, Denice, why don't we just go there next Sunday and find out." A little hesitantly I agreed.

The words *Evangel Temple* sounded a little strange, and I thought it was Jewish, but it wasn't. It was an Assembly of

God church.

We arrived at church a little late and as a result had to sit in the very back row.

As we started singing, the people started clapping. I got tickled and, as a matter of fact, almost hysterical. I was laughing so hard that the tears were streaming down my face. Mama kept elbowing me, trying to get me to quit. Then *she* started laughing. There we were, sitting in that back pew, laughing and elbowing each other. When the people started raising their hands, I jokingly said to mother, "Gosh, mom, all these people have to go to the bathroom at the same time."

Finally the pastor started preaching, and everyone could tell that he was in dead earnest. He would not lean on the pulpit; he would walk back and forth. He'd preach with his fists in the air, a red face, and every vein in his neck bulging. Was he preaching!

As he walked to the right of the congregation, everybody's heads would turn right; to the left, and their heads would turn left. Everybody was following him and holding on to every word he spoke. And then I started laughing about the heads moving, and I was just downright hysterical. But people were so caught up in the service, they didn't pay a bit of attention to me.

Suddenly someone stood up and gave a "message in tongues." I thought, *There's someone from a foreign country.* Then pretty soon the pastor told us what she had said. I thought she had given her testimony and that he was interpreting it.

I laughed through almost the whole service, and I finally decided that these people were just nuts. I was even more convinced after the service was over when a lady came up, grabbed me, and said, "We are so glad to have you here today, sister."

I looked at her and thought, *She thinks I'm her sister? How weird.* I couldn't get over that.

In the car I said, "Mama, that just isn't for me. I really think they are just a bunch of illiterate people." As we drove away, we were still laughing and talking about the people. As a matter of fact, it became our favorite subject every night while we drank our coffee. And did I ever have a time writing Steve a letter and telling him what a crazy church we had visited.

During this time I was still being tormented with all kinds of thoughts of what Steve was doing overseas. I knew he was with all those dirty-minded sailors. One thing I did, thinking it would help, was to give him a subscription to Billy Graham's *Decision Magazine.* Every day I would cut the "daily prayer" from the newspaper and send it to him with my letters. I tried to do everything in my power to keep Steve thinking of God. I was still trying to save him.

One night as mom and I were again talking about Evangel Temple, I said, "You know, mama, you've got to admit that it was fun going to that crazy church." We became more serious and discussed three things we had noticed in that church that we had never seen in another church. The first was that the pastor was excited about what he was preaching. He wasn't just leaning on the pulpit. Also, there wasn't a clock on the wall that you could watch and wish the pastor would hurry and shut-up. The third thing was that there wasn't a man with a pocket knife cleaning his nails. And I didn't see anybody sleeping; everybody was so caught up with the singing.

"Mama, that couldn't be a dead church," I admitted. And then we decided, just for the fun of it, to go back and visit one more time. For some strange reason, it seemed fun to go to that church and watch those people.

In the meantime, my good friend Stacy had returned to Montgomery where she found out that she had terminal cancer. One day they were going to amputate her arm, and then the next day they decided they wouldn't. Finally they decided that the cancer was so bad that she would just be left to die. I was extremely upset and saddened about Stacy's condition.

Then Steve called and asked me if I would come to Europe and be with him. I quickly prepared to leave—even though I wanted to be near Stacy, and I was pregnant.

I knew Steve would be surprised to see me in my

condition. As a matter of fact, in my first two months I gained over fifteen pounds. The doctor had even put me in the hospital on a very strict diet, trying to bring my weight down. I was so embarrassed because I had always been very trim and slim. After the second month most people in the hospital were asking me, "When is the baby due?"

I would be so ashamed when I had to tell them, "No, I'm here as a fat patient."

I had such anxiety in the hospital because I literally felt as though I was starving to death. One night I was so hungry and so full of pains that I woke up thinking that I was going into labor. I rang the bell, and the nurse came in and looked at me. She said, "Denice Vickers, shut up. You're just hungry."

The next day I looked out the door, and a boy was mopping the floor. I asked him if he would come to my room. Then I kind of whispered to him and asked him if there were any candy machines nearby.

He said, "Yes, ma'am, there's one down the hall."

I said, "If I give you the money, will you get me all the candy bars this money will buy?"

He said, "I sure will, ma'am." He went down the hall and came back to the room and closed the door.

I said, "You unwrap 'em, and I'll eat 'em." And in a couple of minutes I had eaten all nine candy bars. That boy's eyes got as big as quarters.

The next morning when I weighed in, I had gained weight. The doctor let me go home!

I gained forty-five pounds during my pregnancy, but it was fun in a way because I had always been so thin that I liked being fat for a change.

In my pregnant condition I scraped up enough money and flew to Germany, from there taking a plane to Switzerland to meet Steve.

I went to the train station in Geneva where Steve was supposed to come in to meet me. All around the station were little flower shops, hot dog stands, gift shops, and restaurants —like a mini-mall. I had a hard time finding anyone who could speak English. I wanted to send a postcard home, but I couldn't decide whether the box I saw on the wall was for trash or for mail. I walked up and down in front of it, thinking, *Should I put my postcard into this box or not.*

I stood there and decided to wait to see what happened. It was very obvious that I was standing there pregnant with a postcard in my hand. A man walked up, and I pointed to the box on the wall. I didn't think he could speak English, but I said, "Mail box? Mail box?"

He looked at me and said in very clear English, "No." He looked very strangely at me.

I pointed to the box again and said, "Mail box? Mail box?"

He let me do this for about twenty times and then looked at me, smiled, and said, "Well, yesterday it was a mail box; I don't know about today."

I exclaimed, "How could you do that to me?"

And he said, "Because I was having so much fun watching you."

I spent the whole day walking back and forth, trying to catch every train to see if Steve would get off. I noticed a man following me, and I kept wondering, *Why is this man following me?* I decided to make sure he was really following me by stopping at a card rack to see if he also stopped. Sure enough, he also stopped. I walked over to the hot dog stand where two boys were, and I thought, *If I stay by them, I will feel safe.*

I stood there for several minutes. Then the man walked up to me and began speaking in some language that I did not understand. I thought he was trying to pick me up. I didn't know why, because I was so huge. I thought to myself, *I need to let him know that I am insulted.* He couldn't understand my English, so I had to let him know with my expression. The two boys at the hot dog stand were listening to what he was saying. They knew all right, but I didn't.

He looked at me and said, "Bonsoir." Then he went on speaking in very soft French. I looked him straight in the eye, thinking, *He's not going to understand this, but he'll know what I mean by the way I look.* And I looked at him, and I threw my head back and very firmly said,

"S-h-u-t-up!"

His eyebrows raised, and he took off running. Those two boys at the hot dog stand started laughing and hitting each other on the back. To this day I don't know what the man wanted. Those boys knew what he was saying, and I guess they also knew what "shut-up" meant.

I stayed at the train station until about eleven thirty that night. My ankles had swollen so badly that they were almost hanging over my shoes. I had been pacing back and forth, and by now I was a nervous wreck. Finally the man at the train station came to me and said, "Ma'am, if he hasn't come in already, he won't be coming in tonight. There's only one more train."

So I called a taxi and went to the hotel.

In my room I pushed a dresser against the door that wouldn't lock and took a bath. I sat in the tub, fearful and crying and saying over and over, "I'll bet my Steve is in France."

I didn't know at the time that Steve had come in on the last train and was in a hotel just one block away wondering where I was.

The next morning I got up and went to the train station. I saw a man who was staring at me. I looked and looked at him and thought, *It kind of looks like Steve, but, no, I'm just wanting to see Steve so badly that any man looks like him.* Then suddenly it hit me, *It is Steve!* He had on a beard and civilian clothes.

We started running toward each other. When we met, instead of throwing his arms around me, he grabbed my stomach just like it was a basketball and said, "Denice, you're so beautiful! You're so beautiful!" He had never seen me pregnant, and it thrilled him to think that I was carrying his child.

While we were together, I quickly sensed that Steve was very nervous. I had never seen him like this. He kept saying to me over and over, "Denice, I can't take it any longer. I can't take another day of this. I can't stand to be away from you." He just held me constantly. No matter where we went on our travels those two weeks, he kept saying, "Denice, I love you. I can't stand being away from you. I want out of the navy. I'm tired of this." I could tell he felt peace when he was with me.

And then in the back of my mind I kept thinking, *He's guilty. The sin in his life is bothering him.*

The whole time I was there, Steve was treating me like a china doll or a fragile piece of precious porcelain. As we'd cross the street, he would help me like I was a little old lady. Everybody seemed to notice how gingerly he was treating me.

We spent several days on the Riviera. We were sitting and discussing what we were going to name the baby. I said, "Steve, if it's a girl, I would like to call her Stacy."

The time with Steve was wonderful. And when I had to say goodby to him, I knew that the next time I would see him would be with the baby in my arms.

Almost as soon as I got home, I went over to Stacy's. She was now bedfast and weak and was skeleton thin. She kept a glass of water by her bed because she stayed thirsty constantly. Her hair had fallen out, and it was so pitiful to see this beautiful girl in such a pathetic state. I wanted to cry, but I knew that I had to be brave in front of her. When I looked at her after my two week absence, I couldn't believe my eyes. It seemed as though she was at death's door.

Whenever I saw her, I tried to talk about pleasant things and tried to get her to laugh. One day she surprised me when she stood up and looked in the mirror. She turned to me and said, "Denice, why don't I just go ahead and die?" Her parents had not told her that she was dying, and neither had the doctor.

I said, "Stacy, don't say that!"

And she said, "Denice, you know I'm dying—you're not kidding me. You know I'm dying, and I know it, and everybody else does."

I tried to change the subject, and she said, "Let me ask you a question. Will you do one thing for me, Denice?"

"Sure, Stacy. Whatever you want."

And she said, "I've never seen a pregnant woman's stomach. Can I see yours?"

She and I both knew that she would never have a child. I said yes and pulled up my maternity top and let her see my stomach. She lay there and laughed and laughed and laughed at how funny my navel looked. It felt so good to me to see Stacy laughing.

Then with tears in my eyes and all choked up, I said, "Stacy, while I was over in Germany, Steve and I talked about what we were going to name our child. I said that if it's a boy, we will name him Steve, and if it is a girl, we're going to name her Stacy."

She looked at me and said, "Denice, you will?"

"Yes, Stacy, we will," I softly replied.

Stacy studied me for a few seconds and then said, "Denice, I want to talk serious with you."

"Sure, Stacy, what about?"

She said, "Remember when we were in Illinois at Great Lakes? I used to make fun of you and didn't want you to read the books or talk about God. Remember when I had those friends and didn't want you to mention God because you would embarrass me? Remember, Denice, I thought you were always too serious about life?"

"Yes, I remember, Stacy."

"Well, Denice, I want you to know I am sorry. And something else, I know now that you are right. Now that I'm sick, and I know that this sounds like an excuse, but I want you to know that I found Jesus Christ as my Savior. I have turned my life over to Him. I want you to know that when you know you are dying, you get serious about these things."

She then reached over and picked up a book, *I Believe in Miracles,* by Kathryn Kuhlman. I had never heard of the woman. She said, "Denice, see this book?"

And I said, "Yes."

"Well, this lady believes in miracles. Denice, she believes that God can heal. Do you believe that, Denice?"

I was the only Christian Stacy knew. And she was waiting for my answer. I didn't really know that God performed miracles, but I looked at her and said, "Stacy, I believe that God can do anything."

She responded, "Denice, I do too!"

When I left her room that day, I was full of joy, but I was also wondering about many things.

The next week I went over to see Stacy again. When I arrived, I couldn't believe my eyes. A hearse was sitting in the front yard. I went into the house, and to my shock Stacy wasn't dead yet. When I went into the bedroom, Ken and her mother went out of the room and let me be there alone with her. She had been a coma for three days. I was sitting there looking at her and praising the Lord. I was saying to myself, "Thank goodness she knows Jesus. Thank goodness she knows Jesus. She's a Christian."

Just then she opened her eyes, lifted her head, looked at me, and said, "Hey." That was all she said, just, "Hey."

I ran to the kitchen and got Ken. I said, "Ken, Stacy's awake!" Then I left the room so he could be with her. Stacy took a big breath and died.

Ken came into the kitchen, put his face against the wall, and wept like a baby. Ken went wild. His life was torn apart. And then I realized that all that criticism I went through during that time had touched Stacy's life, and she knew the way to find Jesus when it was important. If a man gains the whole world but loses his soul, what has he gained. . . . Nothing.

A few days later I went to the hospital and had my little girl and named her Stacy. I asked the doctor, "When will my husband find out?"

And he said, "We'll send him a telegram." Steve was in Greece, and they said it would be a day before he would know.

Three weeks later Steve came off of his Mediterranean cruise and was given leave to come home. We met at the airport when Stacy was only three weeks old. He looked at her and smiled. He was so excited.

We had decided that during this furlough we would stay at Steve's parents' house. In the meantime, Steve's orders were given to him. He would be stationed in Jacksonville, Florida. So immediately we made preparation to move there. We rented a double wide trailer.

And yet, all this time I knew in the back of my mind that something was wrong with Steve. Constant torment was going on inside of me.

One night I decided to give Steve a call at the base to see what time he would be home. When I called, he wasn't there. The fellow who answered laughingly asked, "Is this his girlfriend or his wife?"

I laughed back and said, "Come on, sailor, you know Steve doesn't have a girlfriend."

And he said, "Honey, you don't know Steve Vickers then. I know Steve Vickers, and he knows how to play the field." When he said that, I thought I would die.

Steve *was* seeing other women. My suspicions *were* right. It *wasn't* just my imagination. . . . Or was it? Where could I find an answer? Here I was with a baby, and my husband was out with other women.

My search for answers seemed to be getting me nowhere. I still knew that God had to be my answer. After all, hadn't Stacy found God and peace? But where was the peace for my life? How could my marriage ever work?

In the days ahead I was to find out.

Steve was home from a nine month cruise only two months, and he had to leave again. I was in torment.

9.
The Comforter

About six weeks after my traumatic phone conversation with Steve's friend, Steve came home. He said, "Baby, the ship's going out, and I've got to go on it." Steve proceeded to get me and the baby situated back in Montgomery.

We had bought a little home in Montgomery, but because it would be a month or so before we would move in, I decided to stay with my mother.

She had been visiting Evangel Temple all the time I had been away. And the first Sunday that I was back with her, I was rather excited because I really wanted to go back to that church where all the people had so much fun. Mom had told me she was really enjoying it.

Mom and I hurried off to church and ended up late, as usual, on the back row. Anyone who didn't get to that church early had to sit in the back because everybody else wanted to be close to the front so they could see what God was going to do.

An evangelist got up to give the sermon. He told us he was going to be speaking on the "gift of the Holy Spirit." I had never heard anything like that, and I couldn't imagine what the "gift of the Holy Spirit" was.

As he began to preach, I sat there thinking what a mess my life was in, knowing that one day Steve and I would probably get a divorce. Also, I was wondering what Steve was up to on that cruise.

Then I heard the evangelist tell us that the "baptism of the Holy Spirit" would give a person joy and peace. I sat there like a sponge, soaking in every word he said. I thought, *Joy, oh, I need joy!*

Then he said the Holy Spirit would also give a person peace. And I thought to myself, *My mind is in constant turmoil. Oh, God, I need peace! I need peace!*

And then he talked about the word *assurance.* And I thought of the many times I had lain in bed, wondering if God was really there and if anyone was hearing my prayers.

Finally the evangelist said, "If you want this gift, it's yours. All you have to do is come and get it."

I had never heard of coming and getting a gift from God. It all sounded like a little box all packaged up. He made it sound so easy that right then and there I decided I would go and get it—whatever this gift was.

I stood up in the back of the church and began to weep. *I'm going to go and get this gift. It will give me joy and peace and assurance.* When I arrived at the altar, I cried almost uncontrollably.

Then the evangelist asked something that really "blew my mind." I thought it was a strange question. "Young lady, what do you want from the Lord?"

My mind told me, *Tell him you want joy, peace, and assurance.* But all I could do was look up at him and cry. When I finally began to speak to tell him that I wanted joy, peace, and assurance, another language began to flow out of my mouth. I cleared my throat. Again I tried to say, "Sir, I want joy, peace, and assurance." But I couldn't say it, and once again out came another language. My tongue kept getting all tied up, and I couldn't make sense. I cried all the more.

Then I looked up, and the evangelist was laughing. I cleared my throat once again because I wanted him to know that I wanted joy, peace, and assurance. Then I thought to myself, *This man thinks I'm retarded. That's why he's laughing.* Why can't I talk? Why can't I talk? Why am I talking in this strange language?

For the fourth time I cleared my throat and tried to say, "I want joy, peace, and assurance." I couldn't utter one word in English.

At that point the evangelist looked at me and said, "Young lady, you have received the baptism of the Holy Spirit."

Then I looked down beside me. On the floor was my little brother, Charlie, who was only seven. He was speaking in an unknown language also, and tears were flowing down his face.

Next to him was my little sister Lee Ann. She was about nine. She was weeping, and the language was also flowing from her mouth. And there was my mother also, with tears rolling down her face and talking in an unknown language. Pam was standing by my mother, "speaking in tongues." My whole family, all of us together, received the "baptism of the Holy Spirit" the same day.

My older sister Janice was in Mississippi at the time and had a similar experience thanks to her neighbor who persistently invited her to come to church.

So everyone in our family had received this gift from God at the same time. It was a miracle! We stood with lifted hands, speaking in an unknown language. God had touched our entire family.

When we went home from church, we were so excited. Little Lee Ann didn't stop speaking in tongues all the way home. She would cry and speak in tongues. When they turned the church lights off, we had to carry Lee Ann home. We undressed her and put her to bed while she was still crying and speaking in tongues. We tucked her in under her sheet, and I turned to mama and asked, "Mama, do you think she'll ever speak English again?"

Mama said, "I think so—I don't know." Then we went to get some coffee.

It all felt so good. As I sipped my coffee, I reminisced how I had felt almost as though I had died and gone to Heaven at that altar. When I had opened my eyes and had seen my family around me, I realized that God was indeed a God of miracles. We didn't understand it, but we knew it was from God.

I was thrilled when I wrote to Steve to tell him what had happened. I wondered what he would think of this new experience. Before I received the "baptism," I had been writing mushy love letters to Steve. Now I found another love in my life—a love for Jesus.

My letters turned into love letters about Jesus. I would write and write about how good God was, and I would tell Steve all the things He was teaching me. I'd give him Bible verse after Bible verse and would tell him that when I read the Bible, the pages and verses would jump out at me. I would read the verses over and over and say, "This is for me! This is for me! This is Jesus talking to me!"

I wrote to Steve and said, "Steve, I don't know where the pentecostals have been. Why haven't any of them told me the glory of being filled with the Holy Spirit? All those years of searching, and none of them came to me and told me."

I couldn't understand how people could have this experience in God and not want to tell everyone they knew. When I was baptized in the Holy Spirit, I fell deeply in love with Jesus and wanted to serve Him and have Him teach me through the Word.

He had taken an emotional wreck and placed the Comforter inside to give peace where before there had been no peace. I simply had to tell Steve all about it.

Steve would write back to me and say, "Denice, that's really great what happened to you, but please don't write to me about religion anymore. Please tell me how much you love me and how much you miss me. Tell me what you're doing during the day, and tell me about Stacy. Is she crawling? Is she walking?"

But all I could think about was God. The Lord was working in my life. At last I really knew I had found what I had been looking for. I had found the reality of Jesus. I was experiencing the fact that He could touch me.

The night I was baptized with the Holy Spirit, I cried all night. I kept saying out loud, "God, You touched me for the first time in my life—You touched me! You touched me!" I said it a thousand times that night. It was such a shock to me that I had experienced the personal Jesus. No longer did I only have to know Him by "faith." He had touched me! I discovered that only Jesus could satisfy my soul.

One Sunday I went to the park by myself and soon realized how so many people were out there searching. It seemed as though there was no one to show them the way. My heart went out for all of these people I saw at the park. This was during the "hippie" era, which was taking the country by storm. The park was full, and I looked around and thought, *Somehow they've got to know.*

With my Bible in hand I climbed up on top of a picnic table. I stood there for a moment and then screamed out with the loudest voice I could muster, "I have found the answer!" Immediately my scream drew a crowd. They all came around, wondering what this "nut" was doing on the top of a picnic table.

I began telling them, "Listen, guys and gals, I've searched for almost twenty years, and now I have found the answer." And I told them how I had found Jesus and how I'd been touched by God. I told them about the experience I'd just had in the Holy Spirit. No longer did they just have to believe in Jesus; they could meet Him; He could touch them.

Then one guy from the crowd said, "Hey, this baby's high. Man, she is really trippin'! She's high on somethin'!"

I heard him and looked down and answered, "Man, you're right! I am high! I'm high on something I never am going to come off of." I continued to stare at him, "You take your drugs, but you have to come down. I am high on God." I was really telling him, wanting them to hear about the reality of Christ.

I thought back to my own past life and wondered why no one had told me before about how real Christ can be. I didn't want this crowd not to hear of the great blessing Christ had for each one of them if they would simply respond to it.

Later I wondered if I had ever come in contact with people who had experienced the baptism in the Holy Spirit but were just too shy to tell me about all that Christ had for me. If they saw me on the job, did they simply think, *Denice doesn't need anything. She's funny, pretty, and happy-go-lucky.* I wondered, too, about all those people who sat in church pews Sunday after Sunday and knew Christ's power in their lives but didn't tell others. What would Christ think of them?

After the Lord had done this mighty work in our family, mama often remarked, "Why didn't anyone tell me? We had to go looking for this when there were people who had it but were not sharing the good news of the Comforter."

For years Satan had been trying to destroy us with every form of discouragement known to man. But all of a sudden we realized that God had gotten under us, in us, and a hold of us. We'd talk the Scripture, read the Scripture, and pray together. Night and day we were talking about Jesus and God and the victory we had. We'd laugh sometimes for hours about how free we were in Jesus and how everything had turned out.

Mama wasn't nervous anymore. The Spirit of God through Jesus Christ released her from her nerves. She no longer needed a psychiatrist. She was happy and free. There was nothing negative in her. Everything was positive. God had become her answer. She was learning the Bible.

Today my mother is one of the most positive women I've ever known. People come from all over the city for her to pray with them. And she's mightily used of God. When she shares with people how she tried to take her life, they just can't believe it. She has a real compassion for the unloveable and the hurting; I see the love of God in her life.

I now realize that when the Spirit of God touched me, He really took me out of the "pits." I had known that I was going to Heaven, but I also knew that if things kept on the way they were, I was going to go there with only half a mind. Life was going to be full of hurt.

Now things were so different. In my whole family there wasn't one of us who could keep our mouth shut about Jesus.

How thankful I was that I had found the answer. I found that for which I had been searching so long. I found the happiness, the joy, and the peace that were lacking in my life. How thankful I was that at last I had found the dimension of the Holy Spirit. He would be my Teacher and would fight my battles.

But with the learning and experience of the power of the Spirit of God, I also started finding out who the devil was. And then I realized that it wasn't Denice who was going "wacko" during all the detective work and all the suspicion, but it was Satan doing all that in my life. Here I was with Steve gone and my little girl in the other room, reading the Bible almost night and day. I would lie there and weep at the beauty of the Scriptures as they came alive. God was so good.

I found myself waking up in the morning, speaking in my prayer language and waking up in the middle of the night, praying in my prayer language. It seemed that the Spirit of God was almost continually upon me.

One night I was in the house by myself, and I heard somebody walking down the hallway. I became terrified. My eyes wouldn't shut. I could hardly breathe. I thought I was going to get killed. But I realized that now that I knew Jesus, I had no reason to fear; there was no need for terror to overcome me. So I sat up, and the first thing that came to my mind was, *Jesus, is it You?* I asked this aloud.

I felt such peace. I just knew it was Jesus. And yet I could hear the footsteps like a person walking down the hallway. And again I asked, "Jesus, is that You coming, Jesus?" Somehow I sensed it was His footsteps. So I lay back. The Holy Spirit came over me, and I worshipped the Lord.

On other nights I would dream about Jesus and God. I realized how different I now was. There were no more nightmares. Before I was baptized in the Holy Spirit, I would dream over and over again that Steve was with prostitutes. And sometimes I would wake up so terrified and sick that I would have to go to the bathroom and vomit. No matter how much I had prayed, I couldn't control these dreams. I would cry and be afraid to go to sleep, but now here I was dreaming about Jesus and victory and beautiful things. They were heavenly dreams, and I was sleeping like a baby.

Steve was now due to be mustered out of the navy. We were so excited. He had missed Stacy's little baby stage, and now she had almost grown up, at least what we thought was grown up. She was walking in her little way, and I was getting so excited because he was going to be home. I could tell him all that had been going on in my life, and he could see it.

I knew things would be different. . . .

Steve's mother and dad.

10.
Steve's Answer

When I saw Steve, I was thrilled. His parents were with me, and we were all overjoyed to see him. When he got into the car, we decided to take his parents home; they knew Steve and I wanted to be together.

As soon as we arrived home, I put Stacy to bed. Steve had been quiet in the car, and I knew something was wrong. My main thought, however, was, *Steve can hold me and make love to me. My husband is home.*

As I lay in the bed, Steve sat on the edge of it and looked down at me. He began to cry, "Oh, Denice, Denice, Denice." Then finally he mustered up enough courage to say, "Denice, oh, Denice, I can't touch you."

"Steve, what are you saying?" I cried. "What are you you saying? Why can't you touch me?" My outward appearance hadn't changed. I looked as trim as I had been when he left. I had been a Christian before he had gone away, too.

He continued, "Denice, there's something different about you. You're not the woman I left. Denice, what is it? I'm afraid. Oh, Denice!"

I looked at him with tears in my eyes and said, "Steve, baby, don't you love me anymore?"

All he could say was, "Denice, I can't touch you."

Then, finally, he let me know what was on his mind. "Denice, baby, I've just got to share this with you. Something's changed. I remember when I got those letters. At first you would tell me those sweet things like you couldn't wait until I held you in my arms and we could make love. You told me all of these things that I wanted to hear. They were building me up, and I read your letters over and over again until I almost wore the ink off the pages.

"But then, all of a sudden, Denice, your letters changed so drastically. They weren't love letters to me. They were love letters to Jesus. All you could talk about was Jesus. And within me I've become so jealous of Jesus. Denice, baby, how can I fight God? Jesus is my competition. Baby, it would have been easier if it had been another man or something.

"Baby, I have had such a hard time. On my way home I stopped and got loaded. All of a sudden I seemed to be two different people. Part of the reason I wanted to get drunk was that I knew I was wanting to see you, yet half of me didn't want to see you. I was afraid, honey, of what I was going to face. You've turned into a religious fanatic. Baby, what am I going to do? What's happened in our life?

"Baby, you'll never know what happened to me when I got off the plane and saw you and Stacy. I wanted to run to you and crush you in my arms; but when I came to you, and as soon as I got close to you, I felt there was something all around you. It was as though something was inside of you, and I saw it coming out. And, baby, I felt the presence of something around you. I felt unworthy. I felt unholy. I felt like I was painted dark and black. And when I looked at you, you were pure and white. Even as you sat beside me in the car, I felt so uncomfortable because of this presence around you."

At that I just said, "Steve!" and threw my arms around him. Nature took its course.

Later in the day I very quietly said, "Steve, tomorrow's Sunday. Won't you please go to church with me?" He responded that he would, partially, I suppose, because he knew I had him over a barrel. He had just gotten home and wanted to please me and keep peace in the family.

The next morning we dressed up and, of course, got to church a little late. As we walked in the door, we could hear the "amens" and clapping and people worshipping. I could see the absolute terror that came upon Steve's face as he heard what he thought was racket.

Reverend Vaudie Lambert was the preacher, and he was "on fire." The people were backing him up, amenin' and saying, "Preach it, brother!" What he was saying was so "heavy" that Steve could hardly stand it. One thing I must say about Brother Lambert—his messages never condemn. His message built up the body of Christ and exalted the Lord Jesus Christ and what He had done for us.

We were sitting on the back row, and I heard Steve breathing very heavily. It was very strange, as though he could hardly catch his breath. I turned to him and said, "Steve, what on earth is the matter with you?"

He said, "Denice, I can't breathe in this place."

The second Reverend Lambert gave the altar call, Steve grabbed my hand and said, "Denice, let's get out of here!"

We almost ran out of the church and got into the car. I was discouraged because I had been hoping that he would enjoy the church. On the way home Steve and I were both rather quiet. He turned to me and very firmly but gently said, "Denice, don't ever, I mean *ever,* ask me to go back inside that church again."

After we had been home for awhile, I noticed Steve pacing back and forth in the family room. Back and forth, back and forth. Then he looked at me and said, "Denice, don't you ever ask me to go back to that church again. I can't breathe in that place. I don't like that place. I am never going back. I'll go to any other church in town, but never ask me to go back to that church!"

I suppose the reason that Steve was so uncomfortable was because he had been used to going out drinking all night. He would sit in church and not feel the power of the Holy Spirit. This allowed him to be very comfortable. But the Sunday that he was in my church, the Holy Spirit's presence was so real that Steve couldn't stand it.

After much silence and prayer on my part, I finally got up enough courage to speak to Steve. I certainly did not want an argument on his second day home. I looked at him and gently said, "Steve, I'll tell you what. If you'll go back one more time, like tonight, you'll never have to enter that church door or any other church door again."

When I said that, I thought, *Oh, Jesus, what have I just said? I've given him a reason never to go to church again. I've just fixed him for the rest of his life.*

As I was thinking that, Steve said, "Denice, I'll do it. But I'm going to hold you to it. I'll go tonight but never again." It sounded like a pretty good deal to him.

I knew God was going to perform a miracle that night, and somehow Steve's remark didn't seem to bother me too much.

Again, when we arrived at the church, the people had already begun to worship. Brother Lambert gave a message which was under such anointing that I could hardly stand it myself. As soon as he gave the altar call, Steve jumped out of his seat and ran toward the altar. He literally ran. He threw himself upon the altar, and as he did, his head hit the altar rail. I thought for sure, from the sound of it, that he had fractured his skull.

I immediately got up from my seat and walked down and stood beside Steve. As I stood there, it seemed as though our four years of marriage went through my mind. I thought, *Can he really go a week without lying? Can he go a month without my finding out something he has done behind my back?* I guess in my flesh I didn't really believe he could, but then 2 Corinthians 5:17 came to me: "Therefore if any man be in Christ, he is a new creature: old things are passed away; behold, all things are become new."

But even as Steve was praying and receiving Jesus Christ,

I kept thinking, *I wonder how long it will last?*

Later in the evening Steve shared with me how Satan had been waging a battle in his mind, telling him he was no good. "You're no good, Steve; you're no good," he would hear.

Yet within himself he felt a magnetic drawing to respond to the call of God, and when the altar call was given, Steve just whispered, "God, all of my life I've really wanted to be a Christian." He knew that this very hour was his moment to come to Jesus Christ, and nothing was going to keep him from it.

For days he had been lying in bed crying out, "God, Somebody help me. God, I want to be different. I don't want to be the way I am. God, please, Somebody help me."

Even from the very beginning, Steve confided, it was God in my life and the faith I had in Christ that had attracted me to him. Steve told me that he fell in love with me partially because of the way I looked, but that he was attracted to something deeper in me also. And now he had discovered what that Something was. It was Jesus.

Steve had prayed before, and he had given lip service to God, but this time it was different. He was experiencing regeneration. He wanted all of God. He wanted to be different. He wanted to be changed. He wanted to repent. He wanted to be free. He wanted his life to be changed. He cried out, "Lord, if You still want me, I want You, but You're going to have to change me. I give You my life."

As Steve prayed, he shared with me that God had spoken to his heart. It seemed that within him the Lord was saying, "Steve, I love you. I have always loved you. Steve, I will always love you." And God started dealing with him right then and there about his life.

"Oh, Denice, I have no right to love you," Steve said. "I'm hurting you. I'm hurting you. I'm ruining your life. I'm doing just exactly what people said I would do to you. Oh, Denice, all these years I've tried to hold on to you on the one hand, and yet I've been living in filth on the other. Oh, baby, you've been my only contact with goodness in this world. I don't want to let you go. Denice, I'm like a starving man who has a diamond ring that I could sell. But I'd rather starve to death."

I looked at Steve, and I knew that Jesus Christ was transforming him. And I knew that my husband was going to be a new creation in Jesus Christ.

All the next day—only two days after he had gotten out of the navy—all Steve wanted to do was read his Bible continuously. I would watch him, and he would read the Word, pray, and cry.

Steve soon got a job selling insurance. But the Lord's presence was so heavy upon him that he really had a problem selling insurance. He would go into a home to sell insurance, but right away it seemed that all he could see was their need for Jesus rather than insurance. So he spent all of his time telling them about Jesus and praying with them and bringing them to the Lord or back to the Lord.

After the first week Steve's paycheck was only twenty-two dollars. He was supposed to be making pretty good money, but it became obvious that if he was going to sell insurance, he couldn't serve the Lord so fervently.

That same week revival meetings had started at our church. Steve was anxious to attend and see what God would do for him and in our lives. We were sitting there with twenty dollars that was left of the twenty-two. Our refrigerator was empty except for a jug of water. There was no food in the house at all. That twenty dollars had to pay all of our bills and whatever else we needed. Suddenly it seemed as though the Lord spoke to Steve. He turned to me and said, "Denice, the Lord told me to put this twenty dollars into the offering. And I'm going to do it." And before I could say anything, I saw the twenty dollars drop into the plate. It was gone.

A little bit of fear gripped me as I thought, *Well, here we are—penniless.*

We had no more gotten home after the revival that night when the people who lived behind us (who at the time were not even Christians) called us on the phone and said, "Denice, this is Diane. Have you looked in your refrigerator yet?"

And I said, "Diane, that's a crazy question. Why should I look in my refrigerator? There's nothing in it."

"Well, Denice, just go look in the freezer."

Steve was standing near me, so I said, "Steve, look in the freezer."

He said, "Denice, that's crazy. You and I both know it's empty."

When he opened the door, he found it jammed full of roasts and steaks—not hamburger, just thick, juicy steaks and roasts. They didn't even know our needs. They weren't even Christians, but God saw Steve put that twenty dollars into the offering. That's when God started teaching Steve and me about giving. And from that point on Steve gave more and more and more.

The next day I started cleaning house, and all of a sudden it dawned on me that I wasn't seeing any cigarette ashes around. Steve had been a chain smoker, going through three and four packs a day. He normally had a cigarette in his mouth all the time. I looked at him as he was sitting in the chair and said, "Steve, where are you putting all your cigarette ashes?"

He looked up from the Bible rather startled and replied, "You know, Denice, come to think of it, I don't think I've had a cigarette since Sunday." He was so busy reading the Word and praying, caught up every minute in his newly found joy, that he had simply forgotten to take a cigarette out of the pack and light it up. He no longer had a desire for them. He had tried to quit many times before and hadn't succeeded, but now the habit was gone.

I began to see other changes in Steve also. God was moving swiftly in Steve's life, and he had such a hunger for the Word of God.

Soon after Steve had been saved, he was baptized in the Holy Spirit. I would wake up at night and hear Steve praying in "unknown tongues," seeking the face of God. He would even go into the closet at times so that he could be alone to pray. Our entire lives were changing. We were having fellowship with Christian couples instead of sitting in night clubs with Steve drinking while I sipped on Cokes. Our lives were consumed with talking about Jesus.

Things were going along too well for anything to ever be bad again, or so I thought. But I had one dreadful lesson yet to learn which would tear right at the core of my feeling and life.

11.
God Let Me Out...

Several months of joy swept over us after Steve found the Lord. We had such a happy, wonderful time. For the first time in our marriage it seemed as though I was free and at peace and full of contentment.

However, one Wednesday evening Steve was distressed and came into the bedroom to talk to me as I prepared to go to church. He was red faced, shaking, and seemed nervous beyond reason. He said, "Denice, sit down; I want to tell you something."

The fear that I could see in his face and the way he said it made me think, *Oh, no, he's going to admit things to me. I don't want him to tell me anything. I don't want this bubble to break. I don't want him to say a word to me. I like things the way they are. Oh, God, please don't let him confess anything to me. Let me live in this fantasy world, this realm of total happiness and peace and victory. Jesus, You just tell Steve that we've begun a new life, to forget the past. I don't want to hear it.*

Then I heard this still voice saying, "Denice, listen to him. Hear him out. Hear him out. You can take it. Let him be free once and for all."

Right then I knew that Jesus would bring me through anything that Steve was going to tell me. I believed that it was meant for Steve to share his deep inner thoughts with me. Steve tried to begin two or three times, but he was so nervous that the words wouldn't materialize. Finally, he just blurted out, "Denice, I'm going to tell you some things. And when I tell you, I know you're going to take Stacy, and you're going to leave me. But, Denice, I'm going crazy. I have got to tell you. I've got to get this off my chest. I can't go on like this. I want to walk in total freedom in Jesus. As long as this is within me, I know I cannot be free. I've got to tell you."

Steve had reason to be worried because after our marriage I had told him that if I ever caught him with another woman, there would never be a second time. "One time and you're out!" was the attitude I had had.

He looked at me again and said, "Denice, I've weighed the price, I've thought this through. And I know, no matter what happens, I've got to go all the way with God. And you might as well know, and this sounds hard, but it's the way I feel, that I've got to walk with God first—even above you and my precious Stacy."

When Steve said that, my heart began beating almost out of control. I could hardly breathe. I knew this moment was a turning point in our marriage. I didn't begin to cry. I just sat there and waited for Steve's next words. Slowly and deliberately he began.

"Denice, the entire four years that I have lived with you, I have been lying to you. I have lied to cover up lies to cover up lies. I was going out to drinking parties and getting drunk while you thought I was having duty.

"And, Denice," and he paused and waited, and his lips quivered, "Denice, baby, I have even committed adultery."

Then he named the incidents.

I knew all along that Steve had lied to me and that he had been drinking. I could tell and smell that. But when the word *adultery* came out of his lips, it was as though he had just plunged a knife deep into my guts. I couldn't breathe. It was like I died.

Steve looked at me, waiting for me to scream or yell or cry. I was dead inside. There was no emotion. There was no feeling. No pain. Nothing. At that moment my marriage with Steve Vickers died. Dead. There was dead silence.

He stood there and waited for a reply. Finally I simply looked up at him and said, "Steve, I've heard every word you said. I don't know what I'm going to do about what you've just told me."

I paused and then continued, "Now you listen to me. Don't you come near me! The thought of you touching me makes me want to vomit. Don't you touch me!"

For some reason, in the midst of all this struggle and turmoil and agony, we got into the car (since we were already dressed) and went to Wednesday night church.

Reverend Lambert wasn't at church that night. And when we got there, everybody was at the altar, loudly weeping and crying for some reason. Steve just couldn't go in, so he dropped me off.

I went over and knelt down beside the organ and leaned against the wall. I didn't feel like praying, I didn't feel like talking, and I didn't feel like crying. I didn't feel the presence of God. I felt nothing. I was like a zombie—someone who was walking death.

Just then I looked up and saw the pastor's wife. She grabbed me and looked at me and said, "Denice, I don't know what this is all about, but you need to pray." And I sensed that she knew that something was dreadfully wrong between Steve and me.

"Sister Lambert," I replied, "I don't want to pray. I want you to know I'm mad at God. I've tried to serve God, and now He's done this to me."

Just then Steve walked through the door. He walked right up to the pulpit and said to the man at the pulpit, "I want you to pray for me." So Sherman got on the microphone and asked the men of the church to come up and pray for Steve. At that moment Steve began to sob. I continued to sit there, watching and thinking, *I don't want them to pray for him.* I was mad—really mad.

Then a girl came up to me and got inches from my face and started speaking in tongues. That surely didn't do anything for me. She probably thought she was helping, but instead she only irritated me.

Nothing happened, and as far as I was concerned, I wasn't going to let anything happen. Finally, we simply left and went home.

I was cold and hard and Steve started sleeping in the other bedroom. The very first night Steve came into the bedroom and shook me. I woke up and heard him say, "Denice, Denice, (his voice was desperate) pray for me. God can't forgive such sin." He was on the floor on his knees crying. He was asking me to pray for him, and all the time I was hating him. I didn't love him anymore. I hated him.

Finally, out of desperation I leaned over on the bed and placed my hand on his head and feebly said, "God, show Steve that he's saved and that You have forgiven him."

But at the same time I was thinking, *But You can't forgive him. You shouldn't. Look what he's done to me.*

For three nights in a row that scene repeated itself—Steve coming into my room, shaking me, and crying, "Denice, pray for me. God can't forgive me." And I would lean over and pray that same prayer.

I don't know why I prayed for Steve. I really and truly hated him. But I knew he needed a touch from God. I wanted him to have God, but I didn't want him to have any part of me. However, I continued laying hands on him and praying for him, and Steve would then go back into the other room and go to bed.

Steve continued to pray. I'd wake up in the middle of the night and hear him in his room praying. His prayers could be heard all through the house. During the day, almost all of the time, I would see Steve reading his Bible.

Satan began to torment me. All through the day while I

was cleaning the house or whatever I was doing, I would picture Steve in sin. I pictured him in bed with women. I would become so sick "at my stomach" that I would actually vomit.

I soon discovered that there were three things which would keep me from being tormented during the day. One was reading the Bible, another was playing Gospel music in the house, and the other was praying. If I did all three of these, I wasn't tormented. But if one of those three things wasn't going on, Satan was after me.

One night I called Pam on the phone. I was crying and said, "Pam, I'm dying. Pam, is there such a thing as dying with a broken heart? Well, if there is, I'm going to die. Pam, daddy did this to me, and now my husband is doing this to me. I'm tired of it. I'm telling you, Pam, I'm dying; I'm dying, Pam."

Then Pam started crying. She said, "Denice, I know. I know." That's all she could say because she felt the same hurts. It hurt all of us. So all we did was cry.

The next day as I cleaned the house, Satan began again to put those same pictures into my mind. As I was vacuuming in the living room, I suddenly turned the vacuum cleaner off, threw myself on the living room carpet, and buried my face in my hands. I screamed, and it echoed through the house, "God, help me! Help me, God! It hurts! It hurts! It hurts! It hurts!" I kept saying that over and over again—"It hurts!"

And then I screamed like a madwoman, "God, please, God, let me out of this marriage! I don't love him anymore. God, let me out of this marriage!"

And as soon as I said that, immediately I felt the Holy Spirit all over me. He said, "Denice, if you'll see this man through this, I will give you a man you never dreamed you could have."

I knew that He said, "this man," but I said back to God, "God, give me a man I never dreamed I could have, but don't let his name be Steve Vickers. I don't love him anymore!"

Over and over God kept saying, "I'll give you a man, Denice, that you never dreamed of."

By now Steve had been out of my bedroom for a week. As I lay there, something within me knew that the man God was talking about was Steve Vickers. And then I began feeling the sensation as though someone was pouring warm oil all over me. Even as that was happening, I said, "God, if I have to stay with Steve Vickers, then he has to preach the Gospel." I don't know why I said that, but I guess I thought it would be good if Steve was a preacher. I wasn't willing to pay the price, and I knew it, but I also knew in that moment that in some way God had touched me. So I got up from praying and continued to clean the house.

The next morning when I got up and was straightening up, I realized that I had not been tormented all morning. I had been tormented almost all my life, and I thought to myself, *This is such a different morning. It's unusual. As a matter of fact, the house seems peaceful. This is weird.* Then I realized that I wasn't being tormented about Steve. And I wasn't hurting so much.

I went and lay across my bed flat on my back. I lay there trying to picture Steve in bed with a woman. It didn't even hurt. So I thought, *I'll make it worse; I'll make it more kinky and dirty.* I could see it in my mind, but it didn't hurt.

I said, "Lord, what's going on? It's supposed to hurt. Why doesn't it hurt?"

And then I heard this still, small voice. Jesus spoke, "Denice, you said it hurt. So I reached in and took the hurt away." And then I realized that the hurt was fully gone. God had performed a miracle in my life.

I got up from the bed and began preparing the evening meal. I glanced at Steve, and I thought, *Boy, he's handsome.* I said to myself, *Don't look at him.* And as he sat in the chair, reading the Bible, I glanced over at him, thinking again, *Oh, he's so handsome—he's so neat.*

All at once I thought, *Oh, I love him a lot!* My heart would start beating fast. I felt like a little schoolgirl again, seeing the first boy of her life. I felt myself being drawn to him. Then fear gripped me, and I became afraid that he would notice that I was looking at him. So I tried not to look at him because I certainly did not want to start loving him again. But I couldn't help it, and before I knew it, I was being attracted to him. It all happened so fast—it was like a whirlwind. Everything was happening at once.

Through all of my anguish of the last several days, Steve had been a perfect gentleman. He had not tried to force himself on me; instead, he continued to seek God.

Now passions started building within me, and I saw for the first time the most handsome, breathtaking man I had ever seen. I just couldn't help it.

I went over to the chair and knelt down beside him and said, "Steve, I love you, and I want you to move back into the bedroom."

Steve looked at me with tears welling up in his eyes, and he said, "Denice, are you sure?"

I said, "Yes."

And he continued, "Denice, if I move back into the bedroom, I'm never going to leave it again."

I said, "Come."

We looked at each other. As our eyes met, for the first time I knew we were in love with each other. God had created a miracle. I looked into Steve's eyes, and all I could see was truth. I was no longer looking for a green thread. No longer was there going to be a thread in my life. I looked at him and saw what I had for a husband. I didn't have to wonder anymore about him. I knew for the first time in my life that God had given me a new creation. Even though I had been married to Steve Vickers for four years, I was looking at him for the first time in my life, and for the first time we were free! Free!

12.
Life and Death

When Steve and I finally came together in complete forgiveness and love, my relationships with others began to change also. I realized then how much I also loved my daddy. God gave me forgiveness for him, and now I wanted my dad to know that no matter what he had done or whatever he would do, I would never stop loving him. He is my dad and nothing will ever change that.

Steve had a profound effect on mama and my sisters also. When they saw Steve and realized that there was such a thing as a good man, they were healed within themselves. Mom later came to Steve and said, "Steve, you've renewed my faith in men. Watching your life and seeing what God has done has made all the difference." And from that time on Steve became my family's pastor and counsellor.

Steve also became my counsellor. I had been growing

spiritually, but after Steve and I became one, he now became my teacher and spiritual leader. I began to respect Steve more than any man I'd ever known. I willingly staked my life on him and his stability, because now I knew who he was, and I know who he is in Christ.

Steve had a great hunger for God, and it seemed that every time Reverend Lambert preached, Steve would be at the altar weeping and seeking God's face.

After he became saved, he was more concerned about his parents. At first he tried to "convince" them that they should be saved. He came on hard and with little understanding, and later on he regretted his actions. Instead of just showing the Lord Jesus through his life, he tried to push Jesus on them. We both came on as "holier than thou" toward his parents. But Steve's immature actions were to change as the Holy Spirit taught Christ's love and gentleness.

People in the church began to notice our relationship more than they had before. They also saw the hunger and thirst for Christ that was in Steve. Many people mentioned to the pastor that they wanted the same experience that Steve had had.

One night as we were walking out of the church, Pastor Lambert patted me on the back and said, "Denice, you watch. That husband of yours is going to be a preacher."

I looked at him and smiled and said, "I know." However, Steve did not know it yet.

Again, more time passed. One night as Steve was sitting in the pew watching Stacy and me at choir practice, Pastor Lambert came and sat beside him. He leaned over to Steve and said, "Steve, when are you going to accept the call?"

Steve said, "Why, Brother Lambert, I could never be a preacher. I've been too rotten."

The pastor responded, "But, Steve, your past is all forgiven by God. He sees you clean. What do you desire to do more than anything else in the world?"

Steve answered, "If I could do anything in the world I desire, I would preach the Gospel. That's my desire."

Brother Lambert replied, "Steve, that's the call of God. Just give in and say yes."

Steve started crying, and Brother Lambert started praying in the Spirit. I saw them both sitting there in the pew crying and praying. Steve had said yes to the Lord, and he turned to Brother Lambert and said, "I'm going to do it."

After choir practice I came down from the choir loft. Brother Lambert looked up at me and said, "Denice, you and Steve are going to Bible school!"

I started crying and said, "Praise the Lord!"

The very next day Steve put the house up for sale. It sold immediately. We went over to Steve's parents' home, and Steve said, "Mama and daddy, I'm going to be a minister."

Steve's dad looked at him with shock and said, "Steve, you know there's no money in that."

Steve and his family had always had everything first class. Steve had always been a Cadillac man. Steve's dad had even more class. He looked a Southern gentleman and walked with a cane with a brass handle. I pictured that that's how Steve would someday look because he was built just like his dad.

But now Steve replied unlike the old Steve would have replied, "Daddy, you know I don't care about money. This is what I want." I could see that Steve was perturbed.

Steve's mom sat on the edge of the bed so sweetly, trying as always to keep peace in the family. She was a perfect picture of order. She was neat and pretty and gave a feeling of class. She always reminded me of a person who had just stepped out of a *Vogue Magazine* but who was not trying to be "in style" but rather *had* style.

Steve's mother stood up and looked at Steve. She said, "Well, that's wonderful, son. I understand that Samford in Birmingham is a real nice Bible school." I could tell that Steve's parents were a little bit ashamed that we were "pentecostals."

Steve paused and then replied, "Well, mother, that might be so, but I really feel that the Lord wants me to go to the Assembly of God school."

His mother looked at him and smiled sweetly. She said, "Well, O.K." They never said another word.

His dad commented, "Steve, your mother and I love

you, and whatever you want to do, we want you to do. But I want you to be the best at it. If you're going to be a preacher, be the best preacher there is." That was so typical of Steve's dad. He had quality and drive. When he set his mind to do something, he did it. And he did it perfectly.

Steve and I went off to Bible school and were not there very long when my mother called. She told Steve that his mother was quite ill. I could hardly believe that Steve's dad had not called, but that's the way Steve's dad was.

Steve called his dad and said, "Dad, I understand mom is sick."

His dad replied, "Oh, mom's in the hospital with some heart trouble, but it's not bad. She's not had a heart attack. It's all right. I'll contact you if it gets any worse. I didn't want to contact you until I had something definite."

Steve's dad always dealt in facts. He read *Time* and *National Geographic* and was a well read, factual man. Steve concluded the conversation with his dad and assumed that everything was all right.

However, the next night my mother called again and said, "Denice, Steve's mother is worse than Steve's dad is saying." I immediately handed the phone to Steve. She said to him, "I think you need to pray about coming home. As a matter of fact, I think you need to come home. I'm not going to tell you what to do, and I'm not trying to scare you, but I think it's worse than they think. You pray and see what God wants you to do. Your mother doesn't look good, and I really do think it's serious."

Steve hung up the phone and said, "I've got to talk to the Lord." It wasn't long until Steve came in and said, "Denice, we've got to go," and we quickly drove back to Montgomery.

It was a ten hour drive, and we got there at ten in the morning. First we went to the house. When we found no one there, we went to the hospital. We discovered that Steve's mother was in intensive care. When we got off the elevator, Steve's sister from Hot Springs, Arkansas, was standing there crying. She said, "Steve, go back and see mother right now. This morning mom had three massive coronaries, and they don't expect her to live."

Steve and I hurried to the intensive care area, and mom's room was filled with the sense of death. We looked at his mother and began to pray. No one else was in the room at the time. They were all in the hall crying.

Steve sat on the edge of his mother's bed and stared at her. I was on the other side, looking at her. She was such a queen. We both realized how wonderfully we had been blessed with a mother like her.

As we stayed in the room, I caught myself praying, "Lord, take her easy. Don't let her go through a lot of pain." Then we began praying for Steve's dad, asking the Lord to help him to take the death easy. We kept praying, "Lord, please don't let her have pain."

Steve kept touching her as long as he could. He rubbed and caressed her hands. Both of us were quiet.

Then a thought came to me, and I said, "What is this? Steve, Steve, we believe in healing! There's no need for your mother to die. Jesus can touch her."

We left the room and went outside. We were standing in the hall. Steve's daddy was crying. Steve and his dad hugged and cried. His dad was a broken man and continued to weep. We tried to encourage him, and then we left the hall.

Nurses were busy hurrying back and forth and taking care of other patients who were on the verge of death in this area of the hospital. So Steve and I went into the waiting room where his family and other friends were.

Pastor Martin, a new pastor in town, came over and started talking to us. I said, "Brother Martin, why do we have to give her up? Why do we have to accept death?"

Steve looked at me and said, "Denice, we don't have to give her up. We believe in the power of God and in divine healing. We believe that God answers prayer. Why don't we pray and believe God that she won't have to die?"

Everyone knew that Steve's mother was on the edge of death. The doctor had told Steve's dad to get the entire family to see her as soon as they could because the time was short. Steve's dad had been crushed because it was hard for him not to be in control of every situation.

It seemed as though everyone was counting the minutes

until Steve's mother would die.

It is one thing to know what the Word says. It is another thing to put it to the test when it involves a person you love so much. However, we began praying and claimed that life would come back into her body in the name of Jesus and that she would be restored to full health.

God heard us and answered our prayer. Steve's mother lived and was totally healed of angina heart trouble!

Steve's mother later told us that she had actually left her body in death. She recalled, "I was travelling with white beings. They were travelling and telling me that they were taking me to a special place." She said she started to see a light in the distance, and as she got closer and closer the light became brighter and brighter. She began to see something that looked like a city. She said it was like a planet or something and that light was coming from that city. She said people were flying all around in white robes, and they all seemed to look alike.

She continued with her story that each of the people had tasks to do, and they were hurrying about their business. They didn't seem to have time to sit around and talk about what had happened in the past, but rather they were hurrying here and there, carrying out what seemed to be steady business. She said it seemed as if they were planning for something big.

She said that as she was continuing toward the light, suddenly a shield came down and blocked her. A voice told her she had to go back. The next thing she knew, she had come back to life.

She opened her eyes, and standing at the foot of her bed, she saw Steve and Harry, a friend, praying. After she awoke from near death, she slept through the night. The next morning she was sitting up in bed eating breakfast.

Steve and I had experienced a real miracle, a real answer to prayer, and we rejoiced in the Lord. We both returned to Bible school.

With the passage of time Steve finished school, and we prepared to go out as evangelists and hold revivals. Before the first revival we were so excited that we couldn't wait to get to the town. We were sure we were going to take the world for Jesus. We thought people would come from Hong Kong, China, and all over to hear Steve Vickers preach.

As Steve drove to the town, I read out loud the life story of Smith Wigglesworth, a man who believed God and saw miracles. He had stepped out on faith and God had moved. As I was reading to Steve about this man who believed God, Steve began to weep. He pulled off the side of the road, got out of the car, and walked around to the side. At first I didn't know where he was going.

He stood beside the car on the interstate with his hands lifted up toward Heaven crying and praying in tongues and in English saying, "God, I believe in You. I believe in You. I believe in You, God!"

I sat in the car crying and knew that God wanted us to be children of faith and to realize how big our God is. I began to see that God is as big as we let Him be in our lives. God wanted to use us in a mighty way.

Steve got back into the car and looked at me and said, "Denice, I'm going to believe God. I'm not going to settle for less. I'm going to see God move in this ministry. If no one else is going to, I'm still going to. I'm going to see blind eyes opened and the deaf hear. I want to see the lame walking and the captives set free. I want to see the dead raised." He looked at me again and said, "Denice, are you with me?"

I shouted, "Yes, Steve. Yes, I'm with you!" I knew that he was going to see these things in his ministry. God had already shown me the anointing that was on his life.

My mind flashed back to the day when I was cleaning the house and coming down the stairs while Steve was sitting in his chair studying the Bible. God stopped me at the foot of the stairs and spoke to my heart, "Do you see that man over there?"

I replied, *Lord, you know I see that man over there.*

And He spoke to my heart again, "He's not yours. He's Mine. I'm just lending him to you."

Steve and I hurried to our first meeting in Vicksburg, Michigan. We had prayed and fasted. I could sense the anointing of the Lord on Steve as he waited for the pastor of the church to turn the service over to him. I thought that if the man didn't hurry up and give him the platform, he was going to jump up and take it. He was ready.

When Steve finally began to preach, the Word of God just rolled out of his mouth. I knew God was going to perform miracles that night. When Steve gave the altar call, the aisles were packed, and everyone seemed to respond.

One of the first to come forward was a little elderly lady. Since there were so many others there, I went up to her and said, "Do you have a prayer request?"

She looked at me with tears flowing down her cheeks. She was a godly woman. Anyone could see that. In quite a loud voice, she said, "I can't hear at all out of my left ear, and I can just hear a little out of my right ear. Tonight I know God wants to heal me."

When I heard her say that, I still had very little faith. But she said it with such confidence that I felt sure that God would honor her faith and heal her.

I went over to Steve and said, "Honey, come over here. This lady knows the Lord. She believes that God is going to give her back her hearing tonight."

Steve turned to the congregation. He asked the piano player to stop playing. He said to them, "You all know this woman. You know that she can't hear out of one ear and her other ear is infected. She is under constant doctor's care. I believe tonight that God wants to heal her. You pray with me." At that he placed his fingers on both of her ears and prayed a very simple prayer. He took his fingers away and her head jerked. She started crying.

She sobbed and said, "I can hear! I can hear!" I could see the people looking at Steve and thinking, "This evangelist is really something. He's got it together." But Steve and I both knew that it wasn't Steve. It was God. All we did was step out on faith—faith in a big God Who will do big things if we'll just let Him. That night we let Him, and He did.

After the service Steve was almost too excited to sleep. He said to me, "Denice, do you know that Jesus baptized seven people in the Holy Spirit tonight? Did you see God fill that lady?" He went on and on and then said, "Remember that guy, that real tough guy who came off the street? Did you see him come up for prayer? When he was 'slain in the spirit' I thought his head would crack open. I could hear his head hit all over the church. Afterwards the pastor even went up to him to ask how he felt. The guy looked at both of us and said, 'Man, wow! That was wonderful! Something happened inside of me!' And the pastor said, 'No, I don't mean that. How does your head feel?' And the guy replied, 'Man, what do you mean my head? My head's fine.' "

One of the funniest things that happened in that crusade was when an old man came forward. His name was Justin Case. Steve said to him, "What did you need?"

And the man said, "Justin Case."

Steve prayed for the man and said, "Lord, touch this man just in case." The pastor and his wife started laughing.

Steve asked, "What's so funny?"

"Well," they said, "that man's name is Justin Case, and he thought you asked what his name was." At any rate, God honored the prayer because Steve prayed for him "just in case."

As we lay in bed that night praising God and recounting our experiences, we were excited because we knew God wasn't looking for flamboyant preachers, but He was simply looking for someone to believe Him and let Him be God.

Steve turned to me and said, "Baby, God is faithful. What He says, He will do. I want us to be all He desires. Together let's keep our eyes on Him and follow wherever He leads."

Over the next eight years Steve and I did follow Him. We are continuing to follow Him. I saw a hunger in Steve for things of God. He said many times, "Denice, I want God to use me. There's more. I know there's more He wants to do with me." I would watch him in services as God would use him in such powerful ways in healing, deliverances, and setting captives free. I knew it was all God, that Steve was the empty vessel filled with God, desiring to be used of Him.

Many times I was reminded of the Scripture, "To whom much is given, much is required." God had given so much to us, and sometimes in the ministry when we felt tired and wanted to rest, I would look at Steve and think, *God, I give my whole self to You once again and to the ministry that You have called us to.*

When we had allowed God to change us, God also changed other people through us. Over the last four years, Steve's father, Vic, became ill. I felt a deep hunger for him to grow in the Lord. He and Steve's mother began to read the Bible together and pray together. They began watching PTL Club and 700 Club. Because of these things I saw tremendous spiritual growth in him.

Before he had gotten sick, there were times when we would knock heads together. He had always felt that I was too religious, that I talked too much about God, or that I felt too strongly that God was the answer to every problem. But during his last four years he had changed. Just before Vic died I went to the hospital to see him. People had told me that he had been asking, "When is she coming?" He was afraid he was going to die before he could get the message to me.

I walked over to his bedside. He looked at me, smiled, and said, "You made it."

I said, "Yes," and grabbed his hand and held it tight.

He looked at me and said, "I want everybody to forgive me for anything I've ever done wrong. Denice, I want you to know that I believe everything that you've ever told me. I want you to keep up the good work. I believe in what you and Steve say and what you are doing."

A little later on he said that he was a blessed man to have two sons who were believers. Vic in his last days saw the importance of God being the most important thing in his life.

Steve's father was lying on his deathbed, praising and rejoicing in God. He was even excited about going to Heaven. It was like he was going on a trip to Hawaii or something. Everyday he kept saying, "Maybe today."

We would all reply, "Yes, maybe God will come today."

He waited patiently and with excitement. We were all excited for him also. We were going to miss him, but we saw such a peace in his life. He looked forward to being with God. He was seventy-five, and was ready to go.

When Vic finally died, we all had the victory of knowing without a shadow of doubt that he was with God.

I've never seen a death more beautiful in all my life. He went out into glory. He had a "peace that passeth all understanding." He had his heart right with God. This was such a blessing to all of us and gave us such peace.

On the day of the funeral Steve and his mother and I and other relatives rode in the car behind the hearse. As we drove to the grave site, I sat in the car thinking back on how important it was that Steve's dad had told me he believed in everything I had said to him. That meant so much to me. And it meant so much when he said it in front of other people, the ones who over the years thought I was "too religious."

I thought back to Stacy, my girlfriend, and the times that she had told me I was too religious and took life too seriously and that I talked about God too much. I remembered how the week before she died she had said, "Denice, I want you to forgive me for making fun of you when you talked about God. I want you to know that I've made things right with God, and that all you told me was true."

Then I also thought about what Vic had said about me being too religious. I realized, *Oh, it was worth it! It was worth it! It was worth it! Stacy and Vic thinking I was too religious—it was worth it!* As I looked towards the hearse and Vic's coffin, I knew more than ever that it is God who vindicates—that when we seek God first in our lives, He will take care of the rest. The Word says, "Seek ye first the kingdom of God, and His righteousness; and all these things shall be added unto you." We could have peace both in life and in death. Steve's father discovered that the things in this world are not as important as the eternal things. Before he died, he rejoiced in that fact.

As I look back on my own life to my childhood and my days of fears and frustrations and my loneliness and hurts, the early days of my marriage and the terror of Steve running around and all the torment that put me in, I realize that Christ's peace is able to heal all hearts. There had been so many times when I had just wanted to die. But the day

I looked at Steve and saw that God had given me a new man, greater than anyone I could ever have dreamed of or hoped for, I realized that God is bigger than our circumstances and can take our hurts and turn them into victory if we will just allow Him to.

Now, when Steve puts his arms around me and draws me close to him and says, "Denice, I love you, baby," I can look into his eyes and say, "Yes, Steve, I know. I love you, too."

What a powerful ability we have in our freedom to choose. I thank God over and over that I chose to seek God first and to hunger after Him, and I thank Him that He keeps His Word. I do have a man I never dreamed I could have.

Steve and I with our two daughters, Stacy (10) and Misty (5). Steve currently pastors an independent church in Montgomery, Alabama.